Rock Climbing
the
San Luis Valley

Bob D'Antonio

CHOCKSTONE

FALCON®

HELENA, MONTANA

A FALCON GUIDE®

Falcon® Publishing is continually expanding its list of recreation guidebooks. All books include detailed descriptions, accurate maps, and all the information necessary for enjoyable trips. You can order extra copies of this book and get information and prices for other Falcon® guidebooks by writing Falcon, P.O. Box 1718, Helena, MT 59624 or calling toll free 1-800-582-2665. Also, please ask for a free copy of our current catalog. Visit our website at www.FalconOutdoors.com or contact us by e-mail at falcon@falcon.com.

©1999 Falcon® Publishing, Inc., Helena, Montana.

Printed in Canada.

1 2 3 4 5 6 7 8 9 0 TP 04 03 02 01 00 99

Falcon, FalconGuide, and Chockstone are registered trademarks of Falcon® Publishing, Inc.

Cover photo: Ian Spencer-Green climbing one of the best-looking arêtes anywhere, *Bullet the Blue Sky* (5.12c/d), Penitente Canyon, Bob D'Antonio collection.
All black-and-white photos by author unless otherwise noted.

Library of Congress Cataloging-in-Publication Data
D'Antonio, Bob.
    Rock climbing the San Luis Valley / by Bob D'Antonio.
        p.   cm. -- (A FalconGuide.)
    Rev. ed. of : San Luis Valley. 1994.
    Includes indexes.
    ISBN 1-56044-914-4 (pbk.)
    1. Rock climbing--San Luis Valley (Colo. and N.M.) Guidebooks.
    2. San Luis Valley (Colo. and N.M.) Guidebooks. I. D'Antonio, Bob.
San Luis Valley. II. Title.   III. Series: Falcon guide.
Falcon Guide.
GV199.42.S27D36   1999
796.52'23'097883--dc21   99-29087
                                                                     CIP

CAUTION

Outdoor recreational activities are by their very nature potentially hazardous. All participants in such activities must assume repsonsibility for their own actions and safety. The information contained in this guidebook cannot replace sound judgment and good decision-making skills, which help reduce risk exposure, nor does the scope of this book allow for disclosure of all the potential hazards and risks involved in such activities.

Learn as much as possible about the outdoor recreational activities in which you participate, prepare for the unexpected, and be cautious. The reward will be a safer and more enjoyable experience.

 Text pages printed on recycled paper.

PREFACE

This is the third edition of the guidebook to the rock climbing areas in the San Luis Valley. In the last fifteen years, over 450 routes have been established, mostly on Bureau of Land Management (BLM) land. The concept of this book is to provide a no-frills rock climbing guide to the Valley. For the three major climbing areas, routes are described using photo topos of the cliffs, along with overview maps. For the remainder of the book, overview maps of each area will help you locate the routes. Each area includes route descriptions and directions.

Most of the routes in the Valley are sport climbs with bolts and rappel stations. All the routes are less than 80 feet long. The volcanic rock is very climbable, with pockets, huecos, edges, and cracks. The Valley is an active area, so be aware that there may be new routes in between the ones listed in this guidebook.

Hopefully, all route information is accurate. Any corrections or new route information are welcome. Please notify Falcon Publishing, P.O. Box 1718, Helena, MT 59624.

ACKNOWLEDGMENTS

This book would not be possible without the help and support of my best friend and wife, Laurel D'Antonio. I would like to thank the following friends and contributors for their help and support: Len and Judy D'Antonio, Lew Hoffman, Alex Colville, Fred Martinez (BLM), and Stewart Green. Also, thanks to all the locals who live in the area, especially Mike Spearmen and his family; Ed and Ele Lambert; and the Hicks family. For the new overview maps, I'd like to thank Rick Thompson. Lastly, thanks to you, the climber, who will enjoy visiting and climbing at this unique area.

This book is dedicated to my father, Leonard D'Antonio. My father always was and always will be a constant source of love and inspiration. Dad, I and the family, miss you dearly.

CONTENTS

MAP LEGEND

Interstate	(00)	Campground	▲
US Highway	(00)	Cabins/Buildings	▪
State or Other Principal Road	(00) (000)	Peak	9,782 ft.
National Park Route	(00)	Hill	
Interstate Highway	⟹	Elevation	9,782 ft. ✗
Paved Road	⟹	Gate	•—•
Gravel Road	⟹	Mine Site	⚒
Unimproved Road	= = = = =⟹	Overlook/Point of Interest	◘
Trailhead	◯		
Main Trail(s) /Route(s)	▬ ▬ ▬ ▬	National Forest/Park Boundary	
Alternate/Secondary Trail(s)/Route(s)	‒ · ‒ · ‒ · ‒	Map Orientation	N
Parking Area	(P)		
River/Creek	∿	Scale	0 0.5 1
Spring	⚲		Miles
One Way Road	One Way		

TOPO LEGEND

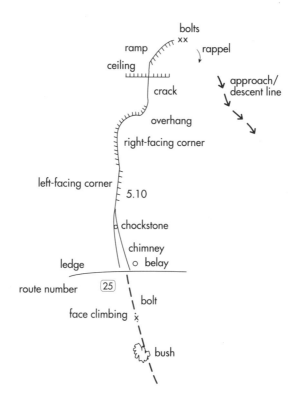

bolts

ramp

ceiling

crack

overhang

right-facing corner

left-facing corner

5.10

chockstone

chimney

ledge

belay

route number

bolt

face climbing

bush

rappel

approach/
descent line

SAN LUIS VALLEY ROAD MAP

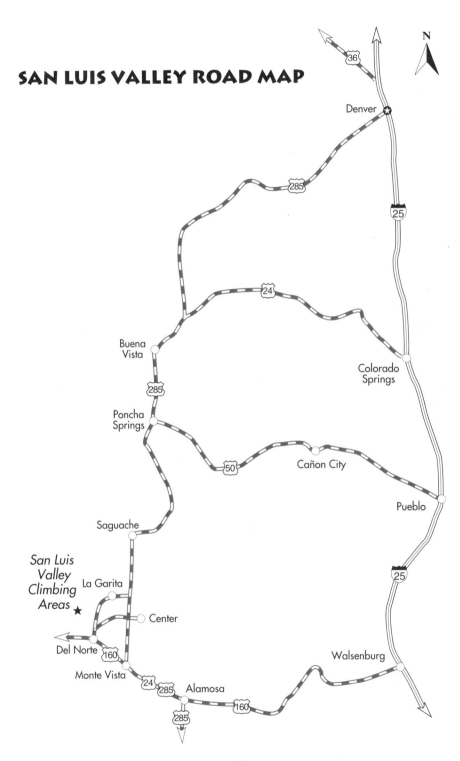

INTRODUCTION

TOPOGRAPHY

When you look at the broad San Luis Valley, you see two different types of mountain ranges. The Sangre de Cristo Mountains to the east are a young range; through heat and pressure deep within the earth's core, this jagged range is still being uplifted. The Rio Grande Rift, simply stated, is a huge crack that extends from Leadville, Colorado, in the north all the way south into the Gulf of Mexico. At one time, the waters of the ancestral Arkansas River flowed down this rift into the Gulf. Nature, however, changes its mind constantly, and as years passed, the waters headed east and excavated a deep canyon, which is now the Royal Gorge.

The San Juan Mountains to the west are the driving force raising the Sangres, slowly slipping beneath them along the rift. The San Juans are an immense mountain range that is mostly of volcanic origin. The peaks and valleys

Dave Pegg clipping on the Penitente classic *Los Hermanos de la Weenie Way* (5.11c).

SAN LUIS VALLEY LOCATOR MAP

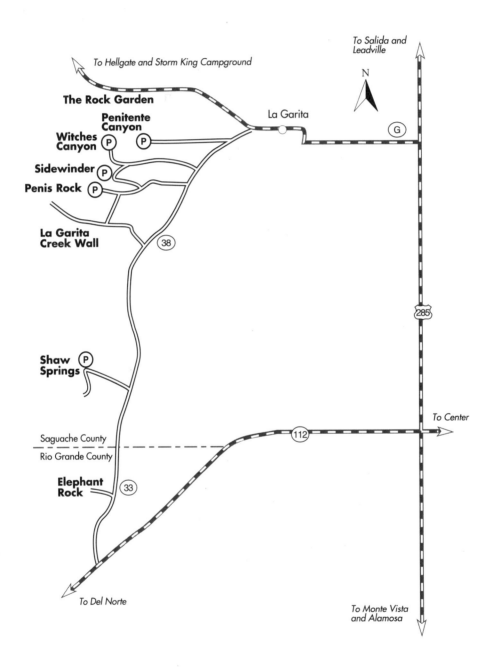

To Salida and Leadville

N

To Hellgate and Storm King Campground

The Rock Garden

Penitente Canyon

Witches Canyon (P) (P)

Sidewinder (P)

Penis Rock (P)

La Garita Creek Wall

La Garita

(G)

(38)

Shaw Springs (P)

285

To Center

Saguache County

Rio Grande County

112

Elephant Rock (33)

To Del Norte

To Monte Vista and Alamosa

generally have a molded look from extensive glaciation, and consequently, the mountains offer easier access, trails, and roads for travelers than the more rugged mountain wall of the Sangre de Cristos.

The flat floor of the San Luis Valley consists of debris eroded from the surrounding mountain ranges. The Connecticut-sized valley, considered the largest in the world at this high altitude (8,000 feet), is a rich agricultural area due to an elaborate system of aqueducts. The area produces potatoes, grains, vegetables, and hay, as well as green pastures that support livestock. The Valley, however, is really a high desert and only receives a scant 7 inches of annual precipitation, making it the driest part of Colorado. Ironically, Wolf Creek Pass to the west is Colorado's wettest area. Irrigation from snowmelt and deep artesian wells supplies the water that greens the San Luis Valley's fields and pastures. Treat this fragile land with respect. Any human abuse leaves long-lasting scars.

GEOLOGY

The geologic history of the volcanic rock formations on the west side of the San Luis Valley, including those at Shaw Springs, Penitente Canyon, Witches Canyon, and the Rock Garden, is a fascinating story. It began some 33 million years ago during an active period of explosive volcanism. Tremendous amounts of ash and volcanic debris were ejected from massive volcanoes in today's San Juan Mountains. In parts of the San Luis Valley and adjoining areas, the ash blanketed the land in depths up to 1,800 feet. You can see this ash formation as far north as Buena Vista and as far south as Tres Piedras in northern New Mexico.

Heat and pressure welded the ash into solid rock, forming a layer called Fish Canyon Tuff. This massive layer of rock cooled and cracked. Erosive forces later weathered the rock into the rounded forms now enjoyed by climbers. These delightful shapes arouse the imagination of everyone who visits this beautiful area.

Other cliffs in the Valley are composed of basalt, a fine-grained, solidified lava. These rocks offer very different qualities from the tuff formation. Interesting basalt layers include the columnar fracturing of a volcanic plug at Hellsgate, northwest of The Rock Garden, and the many cliffs at Big Meadows, on US Highway 160 at Wolf Creek Pass.

HISTORY OF THE SAN LUIS VALLEY

By Alex Colville (Del Norte, Colorado)

Indian Settlement. The first known humans to live in the San Luis Valley came about 12,000 years ago. Archeologists call these nomadic peoples the Clovis Indians from the type of projectile points (arrowheads) they manufactured. Humans may have lived here prior to the projectile time, but this has not been proven. Recording human habitation is done primarily through the classification of stone artifacts. Each culture's tools and projectile points have identifiable characteristics. Most, if not all of the tribes were nomadic, using well-traveled, seasonal migration routes in summer and winter, following herds of game and harvesting edible plants. They did not build any permanent structures.

The oldest tribes lived here during the time of the woolly mammoth, mastodon, giant ground sloth, saber-toothed tiger, and *Bison teloris*. The tribes' stone weapons have been found among the bones of their victims. The Ute Indians, the last tribe to live in the Valley, were relocated to reservations near Durango and Cortez, Colorado, by the white man in the late nineteenth century.

Numerous Indian artifacts and relics have been found around all the San Luis Valley's climbing areas, including rock chips (from making or sharpening tools), scrapers (for preparing skins), spear points and arrowheads, cooking stones, *manos* and *metates* (for grinding seeds and nuts), and pictographs or painted rock drawings. Please leave all artifacts where you find them, and be especially protective of any paintings on the rocks because the oils from your hands contribute to their breakdown.

Spanish Settlement. In 1694, Don Diego de Vargas became the first known European to enter the San Luis Valley. After his visit, there was little intrusive activity by Anglos, except for the occasional trapper, prospector, or explorer, until gold was discovered in the 1870s.

In the New World, the Spanish Empire expanded across Mexico and the American Southwest, claiming all the new lands that were discovered by their explorers. The King of Spain encouraged the settlement of these new territories. Land grants were given to his favored subjects, usually one man or a family, but occasionally to a group of families. These complicated transactions were meant to encourage his subjects to expand the borders of Spanish lands. Some of the more notable land grants in southern Colorado were the Trinchera, Baca, and Guadalupe land grants. After this region became part of the United States, the land grants were split up into smaller parcels.

All of the climbing areas in this guidebook were once part of the Guadalupe Land Grant. This large grant, given to about a hundred families, reached from the New Mexico border in the south to the town of Saguache in the north.

It is interesting to note that the first school in Colorado was formed at San Jose, just east of Del Norte. Among the 14 families who first formed San Jose was a teacher who organized the school. The town was abandoned around the turn of the last century due to the loss of water in the channeling of San Francisco Creek. The bouldering area at Hidden Gulch is just southeast of the old townsite of San Jose.

United States Settlement. During the Mexican War, fought between 1846 and 1848, the United States acquired a vast amount of land, which roughly consisted of Texas, New Mexico, Arizona, California, and Colorado. Although the dates of American settlement follow the acquisition of the territory, the land was given to people prior to the war, which led to a confusing era of legal battles, lost and destroyed records, and misunderstandings.

In the original wording, the land and grazing rights were given to the people, while the government retained the mineral rights. Because of this division of rights, water rights were lost on much of the land, which rendered the properties nearly worthless. Legal battles are still going on in the courts today over the ownership of the Valley's water, the West's most valuable commodity. While ownership of land has also changed over the years, some of the original families of Spanish descent still live on the land given to their forefathers hundreds of years ago.

After the United States acquired the San Luis Valley, the U.S. Army built Fort Massachusetts, the area's first military outpost. The site was soon abandoned because of its vulnerable location, and the post was moved to its present location at Fort Garland. Other outposts were later established, giving American settlers and miners safer access to the territory by protecting them from Indian incursions.

Trappers, usually working alone, visited the Valley. These hardy mountain men trapped beaver in the cold mountain streams and traded with the Indians. Beaver skins were sold and sent east to meet the demands of the United States and the European elite for hats and robes.

Prospectors also filtered into the San Luis Valley, looking for glints of precious metals. Gold was found at Summitville in 1871, and a gold rush began in 1872. The town of Del Norte became a mining supply center that later served the rich gold and silver fields of the San Juan Mountains to the west. Towns began to spring up all across the Valley. The older Spanish villages near the New Mexico border now had neighbors to the north.

As soon as easier transportation on highways and roads was established, vacationers began to come to the Valley to enjoy the scenery and health benefits. Today, tourism is one of the Valley's main businesses. The Valley offers a variety of recreational opportunities, including hunting, fishing, hiking, skiing, and sightseeing. The area's temperate climate makes it a delightful escape from summer's heat in lower elevations. To many visitors, this is "the place to be."

Rock climbing is a recent attraction in the San Luis Valley. While mountaineering and wilderness backpacking in the surrounding mountains were popular for many years, little rock climbing was done on the Valley's many crags. Today, however, climbing is a welcome and much appreciated addition to the Valley's rich history and recreational opportunities.

The author on an overhanging classic (5.12b) in Witches Canyon.

CLIMBING HISTORY

The San Luis Valley is a relatively new climbing area. Most of the routes contained in this book were established in a short period during the 1980s. In the early years, Lew Hoffman and friends from the Balloon Ranch were the main activists, establishing a number of moderate routes in various canyons, mostly in the 5.8 to 5.9 range. Lew, an excellent boulderer, spent most of his time exploring for new canyons and bouldering areas.

In the spring of 1984, I met Lew while bouldering in The Garden of the Gods. In June 1984, Bob Murray and I took our first trip to the Valley. Bob, one of America's most talented rock climbers, established several outstanding and difficult problems. With Lew showing the way, we went to the Balloon Ranch. I managed to fight my way up *SST*, a beautiful, thin hand and finger crack, while Bob cranked off a number of very hard problems. As a result, in one short weekend, both B1+ and 5.12 were established in the San Luis Valley.

It didn't take a genius to realize the potential these canyons offered. During that summer, I made several trips down to the Valley and established a number of routes, including *When the Whip Comes Down* and *Feet Don't Fail Me Now*.

The years 1985 and 1986 were turning points in the Valley's climbing history. Since rap-bolted routes were becoming the norm in many other areas, it was only logical to bring this method to the Valley. Because a few friends and I had the Valley's cliffs to ourselves, we were able to pick off excellent routes at our own leisurely pace. *Lycra-Phobia*, *Not My Cross to Bear*, *Los Hermanos*, *Book of Brilliant Things*, and *Court Jester* were just a few of the climbs done during this period.

By 1987, more and more rock climbers were visiting the Valley to enjoy these magical little climbing areas. Richard Aschert and Mark Milligan from Colorado Springs, Mike Kennedy, John Steiger, and Mike Benge from Aspen, and Ray Ringle from Tucson were all very active in establishing a number of fine routes. The highlight of 1987 was the first ascent of *Bullet the Blue Sky* and *A Virgin No More* in Penitente Canyon. The first time I walked through Penitente Canyon, I realized the Bullet was the obvious route to do. In May, Richard Aschert and I established what was to become one of the finest single pitches in Colorado, if not the United States.

New blood and more extremely active climbers came to the Valley in 1988. Kevin McLaughlin from Alamosa and Glenn Schuler from Colorado Springs were the main activists. In Penitente, Kevin, accompanied by Glenn and sometimes Mark Milligan, established the fine *Dyno-Soar* and numerous 5.10s and 5.11s, virtually doubling the route total in the Valley. Kevin and Glenn's contribution to the climbing scene in the Valley cannot be understated—these two climbers made the Valley into a legitimate sport climbing area.

Shelf Road activist Brian Mullin visited Shaw Springs in 1989. With his belay Mom, he established some great routes, including the multi-day effort on *Venus Groovepusher*. Climbing ace Dan Michael of Boulder added the most difficult route in the area with the technical *Sitting in Limbo* (5.13b/c) in Penitente Canyon. Dan also put up the overhanging *Just Do It* (5.12d) in The Rock Garden. Glenn and Kevin were also extremely active in The Rock Garden, putting up many fine routes, while Mark Milligan blasted up the hueco delight *Copacetic* (5.11b).

In 1990, the action shifted to some newly discovered canyons. Brian, with his wife Melanie, established many new routes in Witches and Sidewinder canyons. The highlight was the ultra-sweet *Spiderbaby* in Sidewinder Canyon. I was active with many different partners in all the canyons, establishing many new routes. One of the best was the overhanging and technical *Jeremy* in The Rock Garden. New arrivals Mac Ruiz, Gus Glitch, and Alvino Pon did quite a few of the remaining lines in Penitente. After many tries, Glenn Schuler got up the overhanging and very thin *DOA* in The Rock Garden, while Mullin finished the razor-sharp *Black Sheets of Rain* in Penitente at the end of the year. McLaughlin continued his vertical assault, firing in some great routes, of which the best were *Double Trouble* and a direct finish to *Cassandra*.

As the pickings got slim in 1991, route activity slowed. Mullin and I did a few more routes in various canyons. One of the best efforts was Brian's overhanging classic *Mudhoney* in Sidewinder Canyon. Later I completed *The Living Year*, a long-standing project in The Rock Garden, which emerged as one of the area's best routes.

In 1992, more new routes were established. La Garita Wall produced several classic routes, with *Vision Quest* and *Pocket Plethora* becoming instant classics. Penitente and The Rock Garden continued to produce several excellent routes, including *Do The Right Thing* and *Sangre Cosida*.

The 1990s has been a time of consolidation in the Valley. With all the best and obvious lines climbed, new route activity in the main canyons has slowed to a snail's pace. The Bureau of Land Management (BLM) and private parties, including the Rocky Mountain Field Institute, have formed a partnership to oversee the future growth and preservation of the climbing areas and these pristine little canyons. The BLM, with grant monies, has installed new bathrooms, tent sites, a water well, and a day use pavilion.

The San Luis Valley has become one of the most scenic, user-friendly, classic, sport-climbing areas in Colorado. You would be hard pressed to find another area that has so many high quality routes, great camping, spectacular vistas, beautiful sunsets, incredible morning light, and interesting and friendly locals. So do yourself a favor—pack up the kids (kids love it here) and the dog, toughen your fingers up, and get ready to enjoy some of the best sport climbing Colorado has to offer.

The Valley is far from climbed out. All you have to do is drive north, south, east, or west, open your eyes wide, and look around at all that rock in the surrounding mountains. It's there for the climbing. Lately I have had the pleasure of developing another area not more than 10 miles from Penitente Canyon, but information about that area remains for a future guidebook.

For me, it is hard to believe that the Valley has become so popular. Back in the 1980s, no one was there. Now the BLM says there were over 20,000 user-days in 1998. From the first time I came to the Valley, I knew this place and its climbing were very special. I guess 20,000 other folks think so, too.

ENVIRONMENTAL AND ETHICAL ISSUES

Lately climbers have been taking heat from all sides for their apparent (real and imaginary) impact on their climbing areas. It's important that climbers do all they can to minimize their impact on fragile lands, such as those on the western side of the San Luis Valley. Keeping good relations with the land custodians is very important.

The Valley's climbing resources are mostly managed by the BLM and the Forest Service. The BLM has done a wonderful job of receiving input from climbers to get a better idea of their desires for the area. It's really our land and they do listen to us. The BLM is taking steps to improve and expand this precious property, for both the present and the future. We wish to protect our rights as climbers and this means playing by some basic rules.

The Valley is a very beautiful and wonderful place to climb and we want to keep it that way. Be sure to stay on established trails whenever possible. Knocking down or destroying bushes or trees just to make your walk a little shorter is an incredibly selfish and ignorant thing to do. Also, deposit trash and waste in their proper containers; better yet, pack it out. Human waste should be buried and toilet paper should be burned or packed out.

The Valley is a fragile, high desert environment, so be careful and use common sense. To obtain further information about minimizing impact, contact the BLM: Bureau of Land Management, San Luis Valley Resource Area, 1921 State Street, Alamosa, CO 81101; 719-589-4975.

Ethics. Okay, here we go! There will be no drilling of pockets or chipping of holds, PERIOD. This trend started a few years back on certain routes (*Cassandra*, *Luca*, *Just Do It*, etc.) and reached its height in the summer of 1990. This behavior will not be tolerated in the future. Any route with drilled, chopped, enhanced and chipped holds will quickly be removed and repaired. Please do not retro-bolt any route without the consent of the first ascent party. Respect the accomplishments of other climbers by not lowering the route to your climbing or protection standard.

The San Luis Valley has a very relaxed climbing scene, but some basic rules have to be followed for everyone to have fun.

Bolts. If you replace any bolts, please use a minimum of 2³/₄ by ³/₈ inch, along with a good climbing hanger. Install only welded cold shuts for non-rap station use. Try to use painted/camouflaged hangers.

Rappel Stations. Please use chains or welded cold shuts for rappel and lowering stations. Slings are prohibited; they are visually unappealing to non-climbers.

Closures. The Rock Garden is closed at the ranch entrance during hunting season from October 15 through November 15. Permission is always required to enter The Rock Garden from the road past the ranch. Ask at the Spearman Ranch across from The Rock Garden.

Toilets. Always use the toilets at the entrance to Penitente Canyon. Everywhere else, stay away from climbing areas and trails. Please bury human waste at least six inches deep and burn or pack out the toilet paper.

Trash. Use trash containers at the entrance to Penitente Canyon. Otherwise, carry out all of your trash as well as anyone else's trash. Please don't leave old slings, tape, Mylar wrappers, soda cans, or anything else.

Trails. Stay on established trails as much as possible. Don't use shortcuts, and drive only on designated roads. This area is a fragile desert environment and it takes a long time to heal its scars.

New Routes. Most of the canyons are pretty much climbed out, so it doesn't make sense to bring your Bosch. New routes are prohibited in Penitente Canyon. If you do establish any new routes, don't squeeze lines or bolt cracks, and place bolts soundly and wisely. Always think of safety for the next party. Use natural protection if at all possible; the rock holds gear well. Say "No" to bolting cracks.

Safety. Always climb safely and intelligently. Climbing is a hazardous sport. Be aware that rattlesnakes are often sighted in the area. Be especially cautious in the brush at the bases of routes and cliffs. And keep an eye on small children.

Birds of Prey. Hawks, eagles and other birds of prey are very vulnerable to human impacts, especially during mating/courtship and nesting season. Please keep your distance from any nests encountered while climbing.

Vegetation. The climbing areas lie in a transition zone between the forested mountains and arid valley floor. Conditions for tree growth are marginal at best. Damaged vegetation often takes decades to grow back. Do not cut live trees for firewood, tent poles or other uses. Stay on existing roads and trails, and obey all trail closures.

Other Visitors. Be courteous. As greater numbers of people come to climb in these unique canyons, it becomes very important to use common courtesy.

Dogs. Keep your dogs under control at all times. This means using a leash when other people are nearby.

Private Land. Ask permission before crossing any private lands. Bulletin boards showing public land status are located at the major access points. If you are unsure about land status, call the BLM office in Alamosa.

Cultural Resources. Removal or disturbance of any historic or prehistoric cultural resource not only destroys a valuable part of our heritage, but it is unlawful on BLM and other public lands. Rock art is especially vulnerable to erosion. Do not touch, deface, or mar any rock art; do not climb over or on it, and do not drill any new routes near it.

CLIMATE

The San Luis Valley's high desert environment makes it an ideal rock climbing area. Climbing is possible year-round with low humidity and generally cool temperatures. Winters can, however, be very cold, but you can enjoy many warm, sunny days on the south-facing cliffs. Spring and autumn are the best times to visit and climb. Wind is often a problem in spring. Expect warm days in autumn. Summer brings a mixed bag. Sometimes the days are too hot for pleasant climbing, although it is easy to find shady cliffs. It's best to get up early or come out late for cool cranking. Watch for heavy thunderstorms and lightning in summer. Nights are often very cold year-round.

CLIMBING RATINGS

This guide uses the Yosemite Decimal System (YDS) to specify the difficulty of the routes. Most of the Valley's routes tend to be in the higher grades (5.10 or harder). This should not discourage any climber from pushing himself. Most routes are safely bolted and protected on excellent rock allowing you to push your limits.

CAMPING AND LODGING

Campsites are available at Penitente Canyon, Witches Canyon, Sidewinder Canyon, and Penis Rock. There is a 14-day limit on camping on BLM lands. Please use existing campsites and fire rings to avoid further environmental impact and degradation. There are no fees or services. The best camping area is the campground at the entrance to Penitente Canyon. There are fire pits, picnic tables, and trashcans. At all the areas, bring lots of water. You can refill water jugs at the store in La Garita.

The La Garita Creek Ranch, located 2 miles southwest of Penitente Canyon, offers discount rates to climbers. Facilities include a sauna and a swimming pool, and the home-style meals are a bonus. The ranch also features some of the best bouldering in the area, set in a lovely small valley at the foot of the La Garita Mountains.

Wills Young cranking the sustained moves on *Cassandra* (5.12d/5.13a), Penitente Canyon.

LOCAL AMENITIES

La Garita. La Garita is the starting point for your Valley climbing adventure. The La Garita Cash Store is the focal point for this very tiny town. It offers an assortment of groceries, munchies, and soda pop, as well as gas and a telephone. The store also serves meals. You can order an excellent breakfast and lunch, along with a great cup of coffee. Stop by for idle chatter, to read the latest climbing magazines, and to hang out with the local ranchers and farmers. This place is what the San Luis Valley is all about. The locals have always welcomed climbers with open arms. Please show them the respect they deserve!

Center. Center is 12 miles southeast of Penitente Canyon. This town features a definite Hispanic flair with low riders and big trucks. Center is a small community that serves the surrounding ranches and farms. Potatoes are a major crop. There are a few bars and an assortment of places that offer gas, beer, groceries, pop, and phones. For emergencies, contact the Center police at 719-754-2442, the sheriff at 719-655-2525, or an ambulance at 719-754-3333.

Del Norte. Del Norte is 13 miles south of Penitente Canyon. Del Norte is the closest place to find a shower, climbing gear, or a motel. The motels and the grocery store sit on the east side of town, while Casa de Madera, the climbing store run by Alex Colville, is in downtown proper. There are also a few restaurants and various bars. Beer, pop, gas, and phones are available at a few quickstops. For emergencies, contact the Del Norte police at 719-852-4027 and the sheriff at 719-657-2731.

PENITENTE CANYON LOCATOR MAP

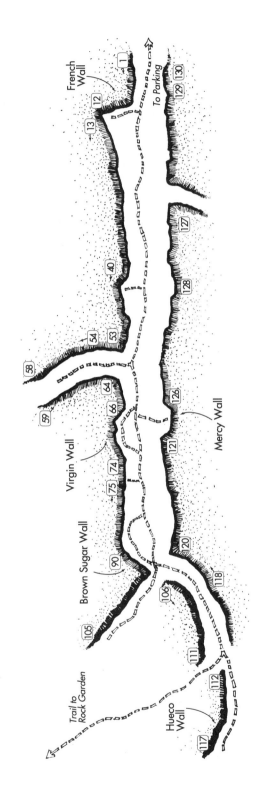

PENITENTE CANYON

Penitente Canyon, a compact, hidden canyon on the western side of the San Luis Valley, is one of the most unique climbing areas in the United States. A combination of easy access, great camping, and fantastic climbing makes for a wonderful outdoor experience. Come and enjoy! You've almost found paradise.

The canyon was named for "The Societies of Los Hermanos Penitentes," a devout group of Catholic brothers who seek to improve their relationship with God. The group was very active in the late 1800s and early 1900s, but now their numbers are decreasing with the members consisting mostly of the aged. It's another unique group lost to modern civilization. The last sign of the Penitentes that remains in the canyon is a painting of the Virgin Mary on the wall left of *A Virgin No More*. A brother who was suspended in a tire by a rope from the top of the cliff supposedly created this interesting folk art painting.

This small canyon, the most popular climbing area in the San Luis Valley, features a superb selection of mostly bolted routes. Minimize your impact when hiking, visiting, and climbing here by abiding by all BLM rules and regulations. The BLM, along with many volunteers, has done a tremendous amount of work in Penitente Canyon. A day use pavilion, new bathrooms, and campsites are just a few of the improvements that the BLM has completed in the canyon. I for one say thanks to the BLM and all the volunteers who have made this beautiful canyon a better place to visit.

Please stay on established trails and minimize your impact on the surrounding plants and wildlife. Rattlesnakes have been seen in the canyon. The area by *Mysterious Redhead* seems to be the place they like to hang out or have a den. Rattlesnakes are usually docile reptiles and only strike when surprised or threatened. If you happen to see a rattlesnake, try not to harm or kill it.

Finding the canyon: La Garita, where the directions begin, is 7 miles west of US Highway 285 via G Road, or 12 miles north of Del Norte and US Highway 160 via Colorado 112 and Rio Grande County 33/Saguache County 38A. From the La Garita Cash Store in the small town of La Garita, drive west and keep left onto Saguache County 38 just after the pavement ends. After about a mile, turn right (northwest) where the main dirt road bends south. This junction is marked "Penitente Canyon." Follow the narrow, dirt road another mile to the parking area and campground. Total mileage from the store is 2.2 miles.

From the parking area at the end of the road, hike into the canyon along the designated trail. Most of Penitente's routes are on the north side of the canyon. Routes are described right to left beginning on the north side of the canyon. Routes on the south side of the canyon are described right to left from the upper canyon.

The first few routes are on the first large buttress on the right. No topos.

1. **Mysterious Redhead** (5.11a) Classic warm-up on the right side of the canyon. 4 bolts. FA: Bob D'Antonio, Mark Milligan; 7/86.

2. **Nature of the Beast** (5.12a) Recommended. Sharp edges, small pockets, and continuous moves. 4 bolts. FA: Kevin McLaughlin; 7/89.

3. **Twist of Fate** (5.11d) 4 bolts. FA: Richard Aschert, Dave Dangle; 5/87.

4. **Twist of Feet** (5.11d) 4 bolts. FA: Kevin McLaughlin; 11/90.

5. **Que Pasa** (5.12d) 5 bolts. FA: Kevin McLaughlin; 11/90.

6. **The Color of Devotion** (5.13b) A boulder problem start (B2) leads to somewhat easier climbing (5.12) above. 4 bolts. FA: Gus Glitch; 7/90.

7. **Camino de la Sonia** (5.12a) 2 bolts. FA: John Steiger, Bob D'Antonio; 10/85.

8. **The Color of Emotion** (5.13a) One of the harder routes in the canyon. Beautiful rock with sustained sequential moves on small pockets. 6 bolts. FA: Dan Michael; 7/88.

9. **Color Blind** (5.12b/c) Small pockets and sharp edges. 3 bolts. FA: Lou Kalina, Kevin McLaughlin; 7/90.

10. **Hareless** (5.11a) Rack: Small nuts and Friends. FA: Dan Hare; 7/87.

11. **To Err Is Human** (5.11d) 3 bolts. FA: Kevin McLaughlin, Glenn Schuler; 5/88.

12. **Abrazos y Chingazos** (5.11c) FA: Jack Hunt, Norman Slade; 3/91.

13. **Tangerine Dream** (5.11d) 3 bolts. Rack: Medium Friends. FA: Richard Aschert, Bob D'Antonio. No topo.

14. **Laura** (5.10d) Rack: Small TCUs, RPs, and Stoppers. FA: Chris Hill, Bob D'Antonio, Richard Aschert; 4/87.

15. **Mission in the Snow** (5.11d/5.12a) A short, classic slab climb. 4 bolts. FA: Mac Ruiz; 11/90.

16. **Mission in the Rain** (5.12b/c) High angle and very technical slab climbing. 5 bolts. FA: Mark Milligan; 7/89.

17. **Mark's Crack** (5.8) Rack: Medium and large Friends. FA: Mark Hoffman, Bob D'Antonio; 5/85.

18. **No Regrets** (5.11c) Boulder up to 1st bolt, or better yet stick-clip it. 4 bolts. FA: Mark Milligan; 5/88.

19. **Whipping Post** (5.11a) Originally a scary 2-bolt route that required mind control, then some weenie with a Bosch came along and sewed it up. 6? bolts. FA: Bob D'Antonio, Mark Milligan; 5/85.

20. **Forbidden Fruit** (5.12a) Excellent! Bring your front-pointing shoes along for this one. Lots of small pockets. 5 bolts. FA: Paul Lanz; 5/89.

21. **Apocketlips** (5.11d) The thin crack just left of *Forbidden Fruit*. Rack: Small RPs, nuts, and Friends. FA: Steiger, Mike Benge; 6/86.

22. **Illegal Alien** (5.11d) 5 bolts. FA: Unknown.

23. **French Lesson** (5.11d) A great warm-up for the more difficult routes to the left. 3 bolts. FA: Bob D'Antonio, Todd Bibler; 5/87.

24. **Glutton for Punishment** (5.12d) Stick-clip 1st bolt and endure hard opening moves. 4 bolts. FA: Gus Glitch; 5/92.

25. **Cassandra** (5.12d/5.13a) Sustained moves and a sequential crux. A great outing for this grade. 8 bolts. FA: Christian Griffith; 7/88. Variation: After the 5th bolt, follow line of bolts up and left. Adds more hard moves to an already difficult climb. FA: K. McLaughlin; 5/91.

26. **Sitting in Limbo** (5.13b/c) The hardest technical route in the area. It has seen very few ascents. Very technical and sequential movements up a vertical seam. 7 bolts. FA: Dan Michael; 9/89.

27. **Dive Right In** (5.12a) Or drop right off! 5 bolts. Gear. FA: Jack Hunt; 5/92.

28. **When the Whip Comes Down** (5.11d) One of the first routes in the canyon. It sees very little traffic due to natural gear placements. Rack: Small RPs and medium Friends. FA: Bob D'Antonio; 9/84.

WHIPPING WALL

29. **The Art of Suffering** (5.12c) Boulder your way over the roof. Easier moves lead to the anchors. 4 bolts. FA: Gus Glitch; 8/90.

30. **Hand Jam Crack** (5.9) Offers good jamming on the lower crux but sees very little traffic due to natural gear. FA: Bob D'Antonio; solo 9/84.

31. **Lovesnake** (5.10c/d) Harder than it looks! Great stemming moves on excellent rock. Edge and stem up the left-facing dihedral to a weird exit move right onto a slab. The anchors are in the wrong place and hard to clip. 3 bolts. FA: Unknown; 3/88.

32. **Prick Pocket** (5.12b/c) Follows a series of monos up the vertical wall left of *Lovesnake*. 5 bolts. FA: Gus Glitch; 8/90.

33. **Stemmorrhoids** (5.12c/d) Excellent and sustained. Technical stemming on small holds. You'll stretch your pants on this one. 6 bolts. FA: Kevin McLaughlin; 10/89.

34. **Rocketman** (5.11c) Take a ride on *Rocketman*. Great route. Hard moves to a large ledge, then more hard moves to the top and the anchors. 5 bolts. FA: Glenn Schuler, Kevin McLaughlin; 5/88.

35. **Bucket Slave** (5.10b) Good and popular. Jam a hand crack, which becomes a groove, to a ledge. After resting, tackle huecos up the buttress above. 4 bolts. Rack: Stoppers and medium Friends for the crack. FA: Kevin McLaughlin; 9/88.

36. **The Sangrador** (5.12b) A hard start leads to great face climbing. 5 bolts. FA: Kevin McLaughlin; 6/89.

37. **Dyno-Soar** (5.12c) Groundfall potential if you blow the 2nd clip. 4 bolts. FA: Kevin McLaughlin; 5/88.

38. **Iron Cross** (5.11d) You will do an iron cross on this one. 4 bolts. FA: Kevin McLaughlin; 4/88.

39. **OPS** (5.11d/5.12a) 6 bolts. FA: Alvino Pon; 8/90.

40. **Dos Hombres** (5.11b) 4 bolts. FA: Kevin McLaughlin, Glenn Schuler; 3/90.

41. **That's the Way** (5.10b) Clip first 3 bolts of Route 43, then head right. 6 bolts. FA: Doug Ranck; 8/91.

42. **Yah-Ta-Hei** (5.10c) One of the better routes of this grade in the canyon. Up the slab right of a deep slot/corner. 7 bolts. FA: Nancie Brabec, Lynn Morrison; 5/88.

43. **What the Hey** (5.9+) The crux is down low. FA: Jack Hunt, Allan Haverfield; 4/91.

44. **Queso Cabeza** (5.11d) Great moves up a steep, clean wall with the crux at the top! 6 bolts. FA: Bob D'Antonio, Doug Ranck; 8/92.

45. **The Wages of Sin** (5.10b) 4 bolts. FA: Jim DiNapoli; without bolts 8/84.

46. **Alien in My Underpants** (5.11b) Probably a small one! A steep start on good holds leads to thin face moves and the top. 5 bolts. FA: Doug Ranck; 5/92.

47. **Persephone** (5.11b) 7 bolts. FA: Unknown.

48. **Loony Tunes** (5.10b/c) A crack start to a hard, edgy finish. 6 bolts. FA: Kevin McLaughlin, Leslie Coon; 5/88.

49. **The Serpent** (5.8) Good moderate that's mostly easy. 6 bolts. FA: Mac Ruiz; 11/90.

50. **Mr. Wind** (5.7) Very popular. The start is the hard part. Think stem. 6 bolts. FA: Mac Ruiz; 11/90.

51. **Mr. Breeze** (5.2) A slabby buttress. Kind of crazy to bolt this line, but it's a great beginner route and first lead. 5 bolts. FA: Jack Hunt.

52. **May-B-Nueve** (5.8) Good route up a slab split by a crack. Follow a crack up left, then step right on slopers and straight up past cold shuts to anchors up top. If you go right of the upper bolts along the crack it drops to 5.7. 5 bolts. FA: Alex Colville.

53. **Captain America** (5.10a) Recommended. Up the buttress on the right side of the slot canyon that heads north from the main canyon. Scramble up a slab onto a ledge. Tricky moves past the first bolt then up huecos. Belay up top from unwelded cold shuts (don't lower or toprope off them!). Rappel off. 3 bolts. FA: Jay Fredinburg.

The following six routes are located in a side canyon 100 feet left of *Captain America* (Route 53). The routes start on the right side of the canyon and work their way back left to the main canyon. No topos.

54. **How the West Was Won** (5.9) Recommended and popular. Pull huecos up the blunt arête to anchors up top. Best to belay and walk off. 3 bolts. FA: Jay Fredinburg.

55. **Concupiscent Curds** (5.10b) 4 bolts. FA: Tom Helvie; 6/93.

56. **Sangre Cosida** (5.13a) A vicious short route that will not only deflate your ego, but destroy your fingertips. 4 bolts. FA: Bob D'Antonio, Mark Milligan; 9/92.

58. **Head Over Heels** (5.11d) Or is heels over head? 3 bolts. FA: Bob D'Antonio; 9/92.

59. **Tao of Gymnastic** (5.10d) 4 bolts. FA: Russell and Karin Rand; 10/90.

60. **7/11** (5.7 or 5.11) Left of bolts is 5.11. 5 bolts. FA: Jack Hunt; 10/91.

61. **Air Jordan** (5.12b/c) On the west side of the canyon and opposite *How the West Was Won*. Expect some big airtime on this one. 5 bolts. FA: Bob D'Antonio; 5/90.

62. **No Intent** (5.12a) A hard crux start leads to fun climbing above. 4 bolts. FA: Kevin McLaughlin.

The following climbs are located 100 feet left (west) of *Captain America* (Route 53) in the main canyon.

63. **The Red Brigade** (5.10b) No topo. Starts 20' right of *Handle with Care*. FA: Andy and Allison Brown, 4/94.

64. **Handle with Care** (5.11b) Loose and somewhat dubious rock. 4 bolts. FA: Kevin McLaughlin, Glenn Schuler, 5/88.

65. **Harvey's Wall Banger** (5.11c) No topo. Rack: Small wires, RPs, and TCUs. FA: McLaughlin, Harvey Miller, 4/88.

66. **Passion Play** (5.11c) No topo. Climbs the face of a wide pillar. The start is hard for short folks. 5 bolts. Variation: Go left after second bolt. FA: Dave Dangle, Richard Aschert, 5/88.

67. **Breakdown Dead Ahead** (5.11b) 5 bolts. FA: Glen Schuler, Kevin McLaughlin, 5/88.

The next six routes are some of the finest in the San Luis Valley. If you are climbing at the level of these routes and only have a short time in the Valley, these are the routes that you should do.

68. **Tanks for the Hueco** (5.10d) Classic. Great name and superb climbing up the steep huecoed wall right of the sharp arête. Begin by scrambling up a slab to a crux layback (5.10d) by a bolt. It's often wet—watch out. Follow pockets up and left, then pull huecos (5.9) to the chains. The first hard move is out of character for the rest of this great route. 6 bolts. FA: Bob D'Antonio, Brian Mullin; 11/87.

69. **Bullet the Blue Sky** (5.12c/d) If you're climbing at this grade, this is the route to climb in the San Luis Valley. A mega-classic. One of the best-looking arêtes anywhere! 8 bolts. FA: Bob D'Antonio, Richard Aschert; 5/87.

70. **Not My Cross To Bear** (5.11a/b) Another Penitente classic! Great rock, great stemming, great route. Do it! 5 bolts. FA: Bob D'Antonio, Mark Milligan; 5/86.

71. **A Virgin No More** (5.12c/d) Another mega-classic with small pocket climbing. Continuous moves with the crux at the top. The first 5.13 in the area. (After the first ascent, some low-life chipper enhanced two holds at the top of the climb. The guy still couldn't do the route after using these tactics. What a slimeball!) 6 bolts. FA: Bob D'Antonio; 11/87.

72. **Los Hermanos de la Weenie Way** (5.11c) A great variation to the original route on the left. Another Penitente classic. Follow the line of chalked jugs up left to some tricky moves up a prow to gain the original route. 7 bolts. FA: Kevin McLaughlin, Glenn Schuler.

73. **Los Hermanos de la Penitente** (5.12c) Great pocket climbing and hard technical moves on small pockets. A classic for its grade. Stick-clip the first bolt, or bring some small gear for the initial crack. 6 bolts. FA: Bob D'Antonio, Richard Aschert; 10/86.

74. **Morada** (5.12a/b) The meeting place. 3 bolts. Rack: Friends FA: Bob D'Antonio, Will Gadd; 9/86.

75. **Friday the 13th** (5.12a) 6 bolts. FA: Mac Ruiz; 8/90.

76. **Freddy's Nightmare** (5.12c) 6 bolts. FA: Kurt Smith, Gus Glitch; 7/90.

77. **Innocent Mission** (5.12b/c) Hard bouldering moves off the ground lead to the anchors and nesting bats. 4 bolts. FA: Bob D'Antonio; 5/91.

78. **The Stimulator** (5.11d) 2 bolts. FA: Alvino Pon; 6/90.

79. **Intimidator** (5.12b) No topo. This is a drilled piece of junk. 6 bolts. FA: Alvino Pon; 90.

80. **True Penitence** (5.11a) Rack: Nuts, TCUs, and Friends. FA: Jim Dinapoli; 6/84.

81. **I'd Rather Leia Than Jabba** (5.11d) I know I would. 6 bolts. FA: Gus Glitch.

82. **Jabba the Hutt** (5.11c) Good climbing on the obvious Jabba-shaped blob buttress. It would be a better line if the bolts were placed properly. 5 bolts. FA: Brian Mullin; 10/88.

83. **Omnipenitent** (5.11b) 6 bolts. FA: Gus Glitch; 9/90.

84. **Santa Cruise** (5.8) Great trad lead! Excellent hand and finger cracks up buttress to a 2-bolt anchor. Rack: Stoppers and small to medium Friends FA: Jim Dinapoli; 8/84.

85. **Reptiles, Lust and Dogs** (5.11b) 6 bolts. FA: Brian Mullin; 10/88.

86. **B1 or V5** You make the call? Hard moves off the ground. 3 bolts. Rack: Medium camming gear. FA: Bob D'Antonio; 6/92.

87. **Unrepenitente** (5.11) 5 bolts. FA: Unknown.

88. **No Sweat, No Vapor** (5.12a) 5 bolts. FA: Kevin McLaughlin, Glenn Schuler; 7/90.

89. **Vapor Trails** (5.12b) Excellent moves on great rock. 4 bolts. FA: Bob D'Antonio; 5/91.

90. **Ordinary People** (5.9) A sort of run-out route up the water streak on the right side of a west-facing slab. Go up left to *Children's* anchors. 2 bolts. FA: Kevin McLaughlin; 4/88.

91. **Children of a Lesser Grade** (5.10c) Thin face moves with a hard upper crux going for the anchors. A small wired nut can offer some extra pro up high. 4 bolts. FA: Kevin McLaughlin; 4/88.

92. **Heaven Can Wait** (5.10b R) But can you? Up a right-angling crack system. Best to toprope this one. Rack: Stoppers and RPs. FA: Kevin McLaughlin, Sam Mills; 4/88.

93. **Jewel of the Mild** (5.10c) A good one. Rounded pockets and thin edges up a progressively steeper slab. 4 bolts. FA: Kevin McLaughlin; 4/88.

94. **Unknown** (5.10c/d) 4 bolts. FA: Unknown.

95. **Luca** (5.12d) Someone pulled the bolts on this route—should be replaced in the future. 4 bolts. FA: Dan Michael; 5/89.

96. **Black Sheets of Rain** (5.13a) Hard moves on very painful holds. Some controversy exists as to whether or not this has seen a clean ascent yet. 5 bolts. FA: Brian Mullin; 11/90.

97. **10,000 Maniacs** (5.11c) Most of them are climbers. Great route—do it. Expect lots of edging. 5 bolts. FA: Mark Milligan, Rich Westbay.

98. **Brown Sugar** (5.11a/b) Excellent edges up the brown wall right of the slabby prow. 4 bolts. FA: Glenn Schuler; 5/88.

The following seven climbs start west of *Brown Sugar* and extend for 200 yards up the north canyon. The trail winds through a dense chokecherry patch. Please be careful and do not destroy any bushes.

99. **Candy Apple Grey** (5.10c) A bouldery start to a slab to a headwall finish on the obvious prow. 4 bolts. FA: Edwin L. Foster, Leslie Coon; 6/89.

100. **Forever Young** (5.12a) Don't we wish! Excellent pocketed moves on great rock. 5 bolts. FA: Bob D'Antonio, Mac Ruiz; 10/90.

101. **Unknown** (5.10) No topo. 4 bolts. FA: Leslie Coon; 10/90.

102. **Vicious but Delicious** (5.12a/b) No topo. 200' left of *Brown Sugar*. Very continuous. Excellent! 6 bolts. FA: Glenn Schuler, Kevin McLaughlin; 10/89.

103. **Pandora's Bosch** (5.12a) No topo. My God, she has one, too! Start just left of *Vicious*. 6 bolts. FA: Kevin McLaughlin, Glenn Schuler; 10/89.

104. **Pass the Shroom** (5.12a) No topo. Probably what they were doing when they did this one! 300' left of *Pandora's*. 4 bolts. FA: Alvino Pon.

105. **Ampiexus** (5.12d) No topo. Short, hard, and painful—another botch job by Gus. 4 bolts. FA: Gus Glitch.

The following six climbs are located in a narrow side canyon west from *Brown Sugar* on The Rock Garden Trail.

106. **Colville Express** (5.11d) 5 bolts. FA: Doug Ranck; 11/91.

107. **Hip Hop** (5.11a) Start 50' left of *Colville Express*. 3 bolts. FA: Addison, Faulkner; 5/89.

108. **Banana Slugs in Heat** (5.10b) Start just left of *Hip Hop*. 3 bolts. FA: Addison, Faulkner; 5/89.

109. **Dogs Delight** (5.10c) No topo. Start 100' left of *Banana* on a rock ledge. 4 bolts. FA: Doug Ranck; 8/91.

110. **Bad Rap** (5.11a) No topo. Start in the middle of the rock ledge. 3 bolts. FA: Doug Ranck, Bob D'Antonio; 8/91.

111. **Animosity** (5.12a) No topo. Start 50' left of *Bad Rap*. 3 bolts. FA: Hillard, Glitch; 7/92.

The following routes are located on Hueco Wall, 200 yards up a small canyon left of where the Rock Garden Trail heads right just past *Animosity*. The routes in this small canyon are short and climb some very interesting hueco-covered walls. No topos.

112. **Pumping Huecos** (5.11) A classic line up a hueco-covered face. 4 bolts. FA: Bob D'Antonio.

113. **Huecos Rancheros** (5.10c) So what did you have for breakfast? 4 bolts. FA: Doug Ranck; 4/92.

114. **Hueco Mania** (5.8) A pleasant route left of *Rancheros*. FA: Doug Rank; 4/92.

Ian Spencer-Green on *Sister of Mercy* (5.12b), a classic at Penitente.

115. **Nueve a Seis** (5.10) A good route up the amazing Hueco Wall. 4 bolts. FA: Doug Ranck; 4/92.

116. **Ranck E** (5.10b) Just left of *Nueve* is this fine route. 4 bolts. FA: Doug Ranck; 4/92.

117. **El Dedo Es la Llave** (5.9) The last route on the Hueco Wall. 4 bolts. FA: Doug Ranck; 4/92.

The next three climbs are located on a ledge just above the trail across from *Colville Express* (Route 106) near the main canyon. No topos.

118. **Apes in Estrus** (5.10c) A short hueco arête. 3 bolts. FA: Tom Addison, Nathon Faulker; 5/89.

119. **Ms. Cool** (5.9) A fine short route up a clean white face. 4 bolts. FA: Tom Helvie; 8/92.

120. **Shady Lady** (5.10a) 3 bolts. FA: Tom Helvie; 8/93.

The following six climbs are located on a smooth face and buttress directly across the canyon from the painting of the Virgin Mary.

121. **Black Jesus** (5.12c/d) Hard moves to start and hard moves to finish. 5 bolts. FA: Bob D'Antonio, Brian Mullin; 4/91.

122. **Sister of Mercy** (5.12b) Classic! Wonderful pocketed climbing up a vertical brown wall. Well worth the effort. 6 bolts. FA: Bob D'Antonio; 4/91.

123. **Schizoid Way** (5.12a) Hard moves to gain the arête! 4 bolts. FA: Bob D'Antonio; 4/91.

MERCY WALL

124. **Dazed and Confused** (5.12a) Up the right side of the smooth face. Move up left and pull over a roof to anchors at the rim. 4 bolts. FA: Glen Schuler, Mark Milligan, Rich Westbay; 5/88.

125. **Sheer Lunacy** (5.11c) Follows the thin cracks on the left side of a smooth wall just right of a right-facing corner. 5 bolts. FA: Kevin McLaughlin; 4/88.

126. **Sheer Strength** (5.12a) Classic! Follows a line of bolts up a beautiful, thin arête. 4 bolts. FA: Kevin McLaughlin; 4/88.

The next two climbs are located directly across the canyon from *Lovesnake* (Route 31). No topos.

127. **Boltergeist** (5.12b/c) 5 bolts. FA: Gus Glitch, Bob D'Antonio; 5/90.

128. **Drill Seeker** (5.9) On the right side of the mouth of a side canyon. Up a blunt prow to anchors on a ledge. Rappel off to avoid trashing your rope. 2 bolts. FA: Karen and Russell Rand.

The following two climbs are located 100 feet across the canyon from *Mysterious Redhead* (Route 1). No topos.

129. **Fixed Nuts** (5.12a) Rack: RPs and TCUs. FA: Bob D'Antonio, Mark Milligan; 5/85.

130. **Boulder Problem** (B1) FA: Bob D'Antonio.

The following three climbs are located 500 feet west on a trail that starts at the end of the day use parking area. No topos.

131. **BBC** (5.11c) 3 bolts. FA: Gus Glitch, Alvino Pon.

132. **Stray Cats** (5.10) 3 bolts. FA: Alvino Pon; 5/90.

133. **The Separator** (5.11b/c) 3 bolts. FA: Gus Glitch, Alvino Pon; 5/90.

THE ROCK GARDEN
LOCATOR MAP

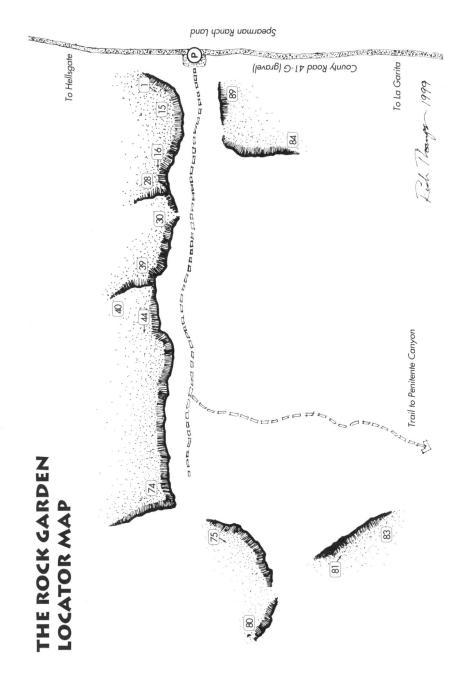

To Hellsgate

Spearman Ranch Land

County Road 41-G (gravel)

To La Garita

Trail to Penitente Canyon

Rich Thompson 1999

THE ROCK GARDEN

The Rock Garden is a quiet and private canyon located just across from the beautiful Spearman Ranch. Mike Spearman and his family are super people who have been nothing short of wonderful in allowing climbers to access The Rock Garden. Please respect their wishes and do not park off the road in front of The Rock Garden. Walk in from Penitente Canyon. The Rock Garden offers some of the best climbing routes in the San Luis Valley. The fantastic views, great rock, and a wealth of easily accessible climbs make this canyon a must stop for anyone visiting the Valley. Again, when visiting The Rock Garden, please access it via the trail that starts in Penitente Canyon.

Finding the crags: The best way to reach The Rock Garden is on a scenic hiking trail from Penitente Canyon. Walk through Penitente Canyon until it splits. The main, oak-filled fork goes to the right (north) and a smaller side canyon goes to the left (west). Hike west up this side canyon on a trail that climbs some slabs to the canyon's north rim. The trail, marked with cairns, winds through open ponderosa pine woods dotted with eroded boulders about 0.5 mile to the south rim of the Rock Garden canyon. Follow the trail down to the canyon floor opposite the cliff with Routes 59 to 71. Route descriptions begin on the west wall at the canyon's north entrance. Follow a trail along the

Kevin Lindorff on *You Can't Blame Lewis*, a fine 5.10c crack at The Rock Garden.

canyon floor to the mouth to find the first routes. Routes are described right to left from here. Total hiking approach time is about 20 minutes.

For an alternative approach that requires permission to park from the Spearman Ranch, drive west from the La Garita Cash Store to an obvious road junction. Go right onto Saguache County 41-G just after the pavement ends. Continue for 1.8 miles to an obvious canyon on your left (south) across from the Spearman Ranch. Park here at a pullout. Hike south into the canyon on a trail. Routes are described right (north) to left (south) beginning on the cliff on the right (west) side of the canyon. Be sure to ask permission before using this approach.

1. **Feet Don't Fail Me Now** (5.11a) The first 5.11 established in the San Luis Valley. Rack: Friends. FA: Bob D'Antonio, Lew Hoffman; 6/84. No topo.

2. **Slapstick** (5.12b) Flaky rock at the start leads to technical moves up the arête. 4 bolts. FA: Kevin McLaughlin, Glenn Schuler; 10/89.

3. **Palming the Porcupine** (5.12b) Named for a dead porcupine found at the base of the route. 4 bolts. FA: Bob D'Antonio, Mike McGill; 8/90.

4. **California Crack** (5.10a) A classic trad route. Rack: Nuts, TCUs, and Friends FA: Kevin Lindorff; 8/84.

5. **Double Trouble** (5.12b) Great moves and perfect protection. 8 bolts. FA: Kevin McLaughlin; 5/90.

6. **Who Dunnit Crack** (5.11a/b) This is another great trad route on almost perfect rock. Rack: TCUs, small to medium Friends. FA: Jim Dinapoli; 6/84.

7. **U2RINXS** (5.11b) The longest and strangest route in The Rock Garden. 9 bolts. FA: Jeff Britt; 8/88.

8. **Static Cling** (5.12a) Hopefully, you will have enough electricity to volt your way to the top. 4 bolts. FA: Kevin McLaughlin; 6/90.

9. **Baby Bun Right** (5.10b) 3 bolts. FA: Unknown.

10. **Baby Bun** (5.11c) Boldness is helpful on this climb. Rack: Small RPs and TCUs. FA: Bob D'Antonio; 6/84.

11. **Baby Bun Left** (5.10b) 3 bolts. FA: Unknown.

12. **Hot Chocolate** (5.11d/5.12a) Continuous moves, with the crux near the top, make this climb a great outing. 5 bolts. FA: Glenn Schuler, Mark Milligan; 9/89.

13. **The Mission** (5.12c/d) This is a short, hard route up a very imposing, steep wall. 4 bolts. FA: Bob D'Antonio; 4/91.

14. **A Sort of Homecoming** (5.12d/5.13a) Excellent! Very technical moves out the roof. 4 bolts. FA: Bob D'Antonio; 5/91.

15. **The Living Years** (5.13b) One of the hardest routes in The Rock Garden. Great position. Well worth the effort. If you are not up for the crux, traverse right after the fourth bolt. 8 bolts. FA: Bob D'Antonio; 5/91.

16. **Pick Pocket** (5.12b/c) 3 bolts. Rack: Small RPs and TCUs. FA: Ray Ringle; 6/85.

17. **This One's for Albert** (5.12a/b) Hey Al, you're still there and I am here. Thin edges and small finger pockets. Excellent. 4 bolts. FA: Bob D'Antonio, Mike McGill; 3/90.

18. **Unknown** (5.11b) 3 bolts. FA: Darryl Roth; 4/90.

19. **Team Genital** (5.6) 6 bolts. FA: Alex Colville, Tom Helvie; 8/92.

20. **The Bottom Line** (5.10b) A great warm-up route. 6 bolts. FA: Glenn Schuler; 10/89.

21. **Court Jester** (5.11d) Great stemming on almost perfect rock. 2 bolts. Rack: Small RPs. FA: Bob D'Antonio; 3/85.

22. **The Terror** (5.11c) 2 bolts. Rack: Medium Friends. FA: Bob D'Antonio; 4/85.

23. **Otto** (5.9) 3 bolts. FA: Kevin McLaughlin; 5/90.

24. **Delusions of Grandeur** (5.12c) Excellent. 100' left of *The Terror*. Follow line of bolts out an overhang to technical face moves. FA: Jack Hunt, Norman Slade; 7/92.

25. **Rocky Mountain Oysters** (5.10) A line of bolts 30' left of *Delusions*. 5 bolts. FA: Jack Hunt, Norm Slade 7/92.

26. **Buffalo Chips** (5.9) The bolted slab 15' left of *Rocky Mountain Oysters*. 5 bolts. FA: Jack Hunt, Norm Slade; 7/92.

27. **Los Cochinos Right** (5.12a) 4 bolts. FA: Darryl Roth, Mark Van Horn; 9/89.

28. **Los Cochinos Left** (5.12a) 4 bolts. FA: Darryl Roth, Mark Van Horn; 9/89.

29. **Unknown** (5.11a) 4 bolts. FA: Kevin McLaughlin, Glenn Schuler; 9/90. No topo.

30. **Unknown** (5.11c) 3 bolts. FA: Glenn Schuler; 9/90.

31. **Come a Time** (5.12d) Technical moves up the arête lead to pumpy moves to finish. 4 bolts. FA: Bob D'Antonio, Richard Aschert; 10/85.

32. **Darla Does Buckwheat** (5.11b) 5 bolts. FA: Glenn Schuler, Kevin McLaughlin; 9/89.

33. **Fine Young Cannibals** (5.11b) The only thing cannibalized will be your ego. Hard for its grade. 6 bolts. FA: Wayne Smith, Glenn Schuler; 9/89.

34. **Pumping Pockets** (5.11d) Recommended. Great climbing on almost perfect rock and pockets. 3 bolts. FA: John Steiger, Bob D'Antonio; 10/85.

35. **Johnny Come Lately** (5.12b/5.13a) No topo. Two ways to do the crux—5.12b left of first bolt or 5.13a right of first bolt. 3 bolts. FA: Bob D'Antonio; 2/87.

36. **Short and Sassy** (5.11b) No topo. 2 bolts. FA: Bob D'Antonio; 10/86.

37. **Gun Control** (5.11a) 3 bolts. FA: Dan Mannix, Jim Vivian; 5/90.

38. **Smoking Guns** (5.11c) Excellent and well worth doing. Rack: Medium nuts and small to medium Friends. FA: Kevin Lindorff; 8/84.

The following four climbs are located in a side canyon 100 feet (north) of *Smoking Guns*.

39. **Three Sweaters and a Football Helmet** (5.12b) Excellent moves with good pockets. 4 bolts. FA: Mike Benge; 5/90.

40. **Unknown** (5.12a) 5 bolts. FA: Kevin McLaughlin; 5/90.

41. **The Deception** (5.11d) No topo. Continuous moves on excellent rock. 4 bolts. FA: Bob D'Antonio, Will Gadd, Neil Cannon; 10/86.

42. **Beers, Steers, and Queers** (5.11c) No topo. 5 bolts. FA: Brian Mullin; 11/90.

The following three climbs are located on a ledge 100' up and right of Route 47.

43. **Tearing Tendons** (5.12c) A very painful, short, hard route. 3 bolts FA: Bob D'Antonio, Brian Mullin; 3/90.

44. **Honeycomb** (5.9) FA: Kevin Lindorff; solo 8/84.

45. **Unknown** (5.10d) Good warm-up route. 4 bolts. FA: Glen Schuler; 8/90.

46. **The Garden** (5.7) No topo. Rack: Nuts and medium Friends. FA: Lew and Mark Hoffman; 6/83.

47. **You're Busted** (5.11c) Great climbing with almost perfect rock at the top. 6 bolts. FA: Glenn Schuler, Mark Milligan, Kevin McLaughlin.

48. **Penal Code** (5.12c) 6 bolts. FA: Glenn Schuler; 7/90.

49. **Crack House** (5.12b) Try not to snort your way up this one. 5 bolts. FA: Glenn Schuler, Kevin McLaughlin; 7/89.

50. **Ready Rock** (5.12b/c) 6 bolts. FA: Glenn Schuler.

51. **The Adam Bomb** (5.12c/d) Hard moves up to the first bolt and very technical at the top. 3 bolts. FA: Bob D'Antonio; 3/86.

52. **I Guano You** (5.11b) 4 bolts. FA: Brian Mullin, Bob D'Antonio; 3/90.

53. **The Black Seam** (5.11c/d) 3 bolts. Rack: Large Friends and quickdraws. FA: Bob D'Antonio; 3/90.

54. **Just Say No to Nancy** (5.11b) 4 bolts. FA: Dave Brower, Mark Milligan; 6/89.

55. **I Won't Back Down** (5.11c/d) 4 bolts. FA: Mark Milligan, Glenn Schuler, Tom Greisan; 8/89.

56. **Rude Mood** (5.12a) Great rock, continuous moves, excellent! 7 bolts. FA: Glenn Schuler; 89.

57. **Long Ago and Far Away** (5.12a) 5 bolts. Rack: Medium TCUs. FA: Bob D'Antonio; 4/90.

58. **Doctor Duane** (5.12c) Can you do an figure-4? 4 bolts. FA: Duane Raleigh; 5/91.

59. **Ligneous Embracer** (5.9) Great slab route. 8 bolts. FA: Tom Helvie; 7/92.

60. **Uncle Lew** (5.12b/c) Named for Lew Hoffman. 4 bolts. FA: Bob D'Antonio, Brian Mullin; 2/91.

61. **Jeremy** (5.13a) Very strenuous with the crux at top. 4 bolts. FA: Bob D'Antonio; 5/90.

62. **When in France** (5.10c) 2 bolts. Rack: Medium Friends. FA: Lew Hoffman; 7/85.

63. **Organic Gardening** (5.11a) Excellent! Rack: Nuts and medium Friends. FA: Jim Dinapoli; 7/85.

64. **Just Do It** (5.12c/d) Great moves and excellent rock. The bolts are somewhat of an eyesore, as are the drilled pockets! 7 bolts. FA: Dan Michael; 5/89.

65. **Do the Right Thing** (5.11c) Spike Lee would be proud. Great moves on excellent rock! 5 bolts. FA: Bob D'Antonio, Jeff Fasset; 5/92.

66. **The Killer Pillar** (5.11d) Watch out for the bat guano. 6 bolts. FA: Schuler, Milligan, Greisan, Brian Becker; 89.

67. **Scratch 'n' Sniff** (5.12b) A hard crux move and very continuous climbing all the way to the anchors. 8 bolts. FA: Glenn Schuler, Mark Milligan; 8/89.

68. **Ya Hoo Serious** (5.12b/c) Tricky moves lead to a very hard crux move! 5 bolts. FA: Glenn Schuler, Kevin McLaughlin; 5/90.

69. **DOA** (5.12d/5.13a) One of the best routes in the canyon. Small pockets and sharp edges add to misery. Excellent! 5 bolts. FA: Glenn Schuler; 8/90.

70. **It's a Schu-In** (5.12a) Only if you're climbing 5.12. 4 bolts. FA: Glenn Schuler, Bob D'Antonio; 5/90.

71. **The Hanging Garden** (5.10c) A great warm-up route. 4 bolts. FA: Glenn Schuler, Mark Milligan; 8/89.

72. **Bop and You Will Drop** (5.11a) A long runout on dubious rock. 1 bolt. FA: Bob D'Antonio; 8/84.

73. **Short and Shitty** (5.12a) A short, nasty, little crack that's probably not worth the effort. 2 bolts. Rack: Medium Friends. FA: Bob D'Antonio; 3/90.

Jack Hunt just pulled the overhang on The Rock Garden's *Delusions of Grandeur* (5.12c).

The next route is tucked into a small side canyon, 100 feet left (north) of *Short and Shitty*.

74. **BM Was Here** (5.12b) No topo. Excellent and very technical. 4 bolts. FA: Bob D'Antonio, Bob Murray; 4/90.

The following five climbs are located 300 feet west of *DOA* and start on a ledge 50 feet above from the trail.

75. **Achilles Last Stand** (5.11d) 3 bolts. FA: Gus Glitch; 5/97.

76. **The Shield Of Achilles** (5.13a) More like a V7 boulder problem. Crack the start and you're home free. 3 bolts. FA: Mark Milligan; 5/90.

77. **Copacetic** (5.11b) Great stemming moves up an overhanging, pocketed wall. 4 bolts. FA: Mark Milligan, Wayne Smith.

78. **Jugalicious** (5.10a) Starts just left of *Copacetic*. 4 bolts FA: Monica Browne; 5/97.

79. **Ninos y Viejos** (5.9) 6 bolts. FA: Alex Colville; 6/96.

80. **Payback** (5.12c/d) No topo. Good climbing up to a small roof and the crux. 4 bolts. FA: Bob D'Antonio; 2/99.

81. **You Can't Blame Lewis** (5.10c) No topo. A fine crack across the canyon from *Copacetic* (northeast). Rack: Medium Friends. FA: Bob D'Antonio; 8/85.

82. **Unknown** (5.10d) No topo. A wall with bolts just left of *Lewis*. 4 bolts. FA: Unknown.

83. **No Respect for Age** (5.8) No topo. 5 bolts. FA: Alex Colville; 8/92.

The following six climbs are located 300 feet east of *The Terror* (Route 22), on the opposite (east) side of the canyon. The climbs start in the back of the canyon and work out to the main trail. No topos.

84. **Big Brett the Baker's Buddy** (5.9) The right-hand of two routes on a small wall. 3 bolts. FA: Tom Helvie, Cesar Perez; 6/96.

85. **Wallrus** (5.8) The left-hand route. 3 bolts. FA: Tom Helvie, Cesar Perez; 6/96.

86. **Fed Ex** (5.10a) Follow a line of bolts up to a diagonal crack and the top. FA: Tom Helvie, Cesar Perez; 6/96.

87. **I+CN'?** (5.6) A short route up a face down right of *Lycra-Phobia*. FA: Alex Colville, Anna Kekesi; 6/96.

88. **Lycra-Phobia** (5.12b/c) 1 pin. Rack: Small and medium Friends. FA: Bob D'Antonio; 4/85.

89. **Standing on the Corner of the Third World** (5.12b/c) Just off the trail and down and left of *Lycra-Phobia*. A hard crux at the start leads to good pockets and the finish. 3 bolts. FA: Bob D'Antonio, Brian Mullin; 2/90.

The next two routes are located on a pinnacle directly across from *U2RINXS* (Route 7) near the head of the canyon. No topo.

90. **Busting Loose** (5.12a) 3 bolts. FA: Bob D'Antonio; 5/92.

91. **Bust A Move** (5.12a/b) 4 bolts. FA: Schuler, Kevin McLaughlin, Mark Milligan; 10/89.

WITCHES CANYON LOCATOR MAP

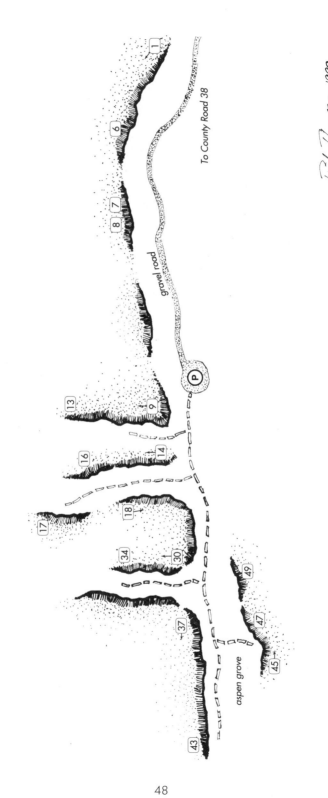

To County Road 38

gravel road

P

aspen grove

Reh Young 1999

WITCHES CANYON

Witches Canyon, hidden in the foothills southwest of Penitente Canyon, was named for a strange rock outcrop that resembles a giant eye. The canyon is still fairly remote and unknown to most visiting climbers. This isolation keeps it uncrowded and quiet. The haunting cliffs and hidden side canyons are inhabited only by witches and noisy ravens—watch out on dark nights.

The cliffs tend to be short but laced with excellent routes. A few routes lie near the mouth of the canyon, but most are located beyond the end of the road. The vast majority of the routes are oriented east and west, so the canyon is a great place to play hide and seek with the sun. The routes vary in difficulty from 5.9 to 5.13, with many in the 5.10 range, making Witches Canyon a nice destination for moderate climbers.

The main canyon runs in an east-to-west direction and parallels a dry creek bed. The canyon receives sun most of the day. Several small canyons that branch off the main canyon offer some of the best routes. Also, there is an assortment of good and fun boulder problems along the road in the canyon, especially on the southeast side almost halfway into the canyon. Look for some excellent, long hueco problems. Boulderers will enjoy exploring this pristine area with only a chalk bag and crash pad.

Finding the canyon: Zero your odometer at the turnoff for Penitente Canyon, which is a mile west of the La Garita Cash Store, and head south on the main road (Saguache County 38). At 0.6 mile, look for a rough road that heads due west and a sign marked "Witches Canyon." Turn right here and follow the road west. At 1.5 miles, veer left, then at about 1.8 miles, drop downhill and turn right into Witches Canyon. The road continues another 0.5 mile, with routes alongside it. The road is a bit rough, but two-wheel-drive cars can make it. High clearance is advisable. Please don't park in the middle of the road and block other traffic. The best parking area is at the road's end. The BLM is going to close the road into Witches Canyon sometime in the future. You can access Witches Canyon by walking cross-country from the Penitente Campground. As of 1999, the road is still open.

1. **Unknown** (5.9) A short bolted route just right of *Squidbelly*. 3 bolts.

2. **Squidbelly Phlegmfoot** (5.10c) The second route in the canyon on the north side of the road. Climb the obvious, huecoed tombstone. 3 bolts. FA: Brian Mullin, Melanie Tuttle; 3/90.

3. **Unknown** (5.9) Follow a line of bolts up a hueco-studded face. 4 bolts.

4. **Unknown** (5.9) Bolted face just right of *Eyes of the Witch*. 4 bolts.

5. **Eyes of the Witch** (5.12) 65' left of *Squidbelly*. Start up a thin seam and go left up to the eyes. Hueco and edges. 4 bolts. FA: Bob D'Antonio; 4/91.

6. **Dashboard Saints** (5.11b) Next to a tree, 75' left of *Squidbelly*. Crack to hueco dishes. 4 bolts. FA: Brian Mullin; 3/90. **Variation:** Go left at the second bolt (5.9).

7. **Evil Barbecue** (5.10b) No topo. By a parking area just before road first crosses a dry streambed. Huecos. 3 bolts. FA: Brian Mullin; 3/90.

8. **Lunge for Jesus** (5.11b) No topo. 125' left of *Evil Barbecue*. Boulder problem start to great jug roof. 4 bolts. FA: Brian Mullin; 3/90.

The next four climbs are located in a small canyon up and right from the parking area at the end of the road.

9. **Drug Test** (5.11a) The first of four high-quality short routes. The first route on a short, pocketed, overhanging wall. 3 bolts. FA: Brian Mullin; 4/90.

10. **Laughing at the Ground** (5.12b) Left of *Drug Test*. Thin pockets and edges—watch your creaking tendons! 4 bolts. FA: Brian Mullin; 4/90.

11. **Project** (5.13a) Second route left of *Drug Test*.

Kevin Branford making a move on *Lunge For Jesus* (5.11b) in Witches Canyon.

12. **Horseshoes and Grenades** (5.12c) "Almost" doesn't count on this one. A lot of hard moves on sharp holds and great rock. 4 bolts. FA: Brian Mullin, Bob D'Antonio; 5/92.

13. **Tall Dwarfs** (5.9) No topo. In a small canyon on the right just where the road ends. Route is by a tall evergreen. 3 bolts. FA: Brian Mullin, Melanie Tuttle; 5/90.

The following four climbs are located in a beautiful small canyon situated just before *Drugs Are Nice* (Route 20). This canyon has some of the most beautiful old-growth ponderosa pine trees in the San Luis Valley. No topos.

14. **Screaming Trees** (5.11d) Go right past *Drugs Are Nice* into a small canyon. This route is just right of a large pine tree. Creep up a slab start to a thin face. 4 bolts. FA: Brian Mullin; 2/91.

15. **Sonic Rumble Hammer** (5.12a/b) Right of a tall evergreen, 100' northwest of *Screaming Trees*. 4 bolts. FA: Brian Mullin, Melanie Tuttle; 5/90.

16. **Step Out of Time** (5.12a) Follow the trail farther west into the canyon to the route on the right, just right of a large pine tree. Incredible hueco dishes. 5 bolts. FA: Brian Mullin; 6/90.

17. **In Step, Out of Rhythm** (5.12d) The route is located at the end of the canyon on a beautiful, pocketed wall on the left. (FA: Bob D'Antonio 5/93)

18. **Psychodaisies** (5.12b) Somewhat contrived because you can easily stem behind you to make the route easier. Second route right of *Drugs Are Nice*. Very thin face, easier upper face. 5 bolts. FA: Brian Mullin; 4/90.

The Witches Eye

19. **Fade Out** (5.10d/5.11a) Right of *Drugs Are Nice*. Hueco start to pockets and edges. 3 bolts. FA: Brian Mullin, Melanie Tuttle; 3/91.

20. **Drugs Are Nice** (5.10a) Where were you in the 60s? Faces directly east and toward the road. Excellent slab and face climbing. 4 bolts. FA: Brian Mullin, Melanie Tuttle; 4/90.

21. **Woof** (5.10c) No topo. Follow the trail left to a large roof. Follow line of bolts out the right side of the roof. 4 bolts. FA: Jack Hunt.

22. **Egotonio** (5.12c) My ego is not really that big. No topo. The route goes out the left side of the roof. Follow the face up to the roof and the crux. The formation looks like a bear's head. A wild roof. 5 bolts. FA: Bob D'Antonio; 5/90.

23. **Show Her Your Stem** (5.11b/c) I will if you will. Corner crack 50' past *Egotonio*. 1 bolt. Rack: Small to medium TCUs. FA: Brian Mullin; 7/90.

24. **Plump and Luscious** (5.11c/d) Left of *Show Her Your Stem*. Nice slab start. 4 bolts. FA: Brian Mullin, Melanie Tuttle; 4/90.

25. **Slimier** (5.10d) 20' west and 10' back of *Stem*. Small, rounded holds up to a slab finish. 3 bolts. FA: Brian Mullin, Melanie Tuttle; 5/90.

26. **Jesus Liquid** (5.10d) Left of *Slimier*. Fun bulge with big holds. 3 bolts. FA: Brian Mullin, Melanie Tuttle; 5/90.

27. **Cracks 'R' Us** (5.10) Second route left of *Slimier*. Layback crack. 2 bolts. Rack: TCUs and wires. FA: Bob D'Antonio.

28. **Razor Hueco Arête** (5.10a) No topo. Obvious hueco arête 50' west of *Slimier*. Nice huecos and jugs. 3 bolts. FA: Brian Mullin, Melanie Tuttle; 4/90.

29. **Waitress in the Sky** (5.8) No topo. Crack to the left and on the other side of *Razor*. Use the rap station on *Razor*. Rack: Medium TCUs. FA: Brian Mullin, Melanie Tuttle; 7/90.

30. **Witches' Tit** (5.12b) Classic! The first bolted route left of *Razor Hueco Arête* on an overhanging wall. 4 bolts. FA: Bob D'Antonio, Chris Van Diver; 90.

31. **Weave Your Spell** (5.12a) Another classic route on this beautiful wall. The second bolted route left of the *Razor Hueco Arête* on large wall. 3 bolts. FA: Bob D'Antonio; 90.

32. **Spellbound** (5.12c/d) No daydreaming on this route. The crux is halfway up on small, sharp holds. FA: Bob D'Antonio; 5/95.

33. **Witching Hour** (5.11c) No topo. First climbed on Halloween day. A crack line 15' left of *Spellbound* on large wall. Just below obvious Witch's Eye outcropping. Layback up crack and climb the face to the eye. 4 bolts. FA: Mike McGill, Bob D'Antonio; 10/31/90.

34. **Friend of the Devil** (5.11c) No topo. Left of *Witching Hour*. Brown and tan wall. 4 bolts. FA: Bob D'Antonio, Cameron Burns; 4/90.

35. **Deny Everything** (5.11b) No topo. 175' west of *Razor Hueco Arête* by the creek. Slab to face. 4 bolts. FA: Brian Mullin; 10/90.

36. **Rubber Legs** (5.12a/b) No topo. 450' past *Razor Hueco Arête*. Go right at small ledge and up to the start. Overhanging edges. 4 bolts. FA: Brian Mullin; 3/91.

To locate the next seven routes, follow the creekbed straight back into this small, beautiful aspen-filled canyon. Some of the best routes in the canyon are located back in this area. No topos.

37. **The Golden Egg** (5.8) 450' past *Razor Hueco Arête*; go right at small rock ledge, then another 250'. Obvious V-shaped slab crack. Loose finish. 2 bolts. FA: Tim Canon, Cliff Mallory 5/90.

38. **A Grim Fairy Tale** (5.11a/b) 60' left of *The Golden Egg*. 4 bolts. (FA: Cliff Mallory, Tim Canon, Kevin McLaughlin 5/90.

39. **Project** (5.12d/5.13a) Second route right of *Purple Haze* on large wall.

40. **Ubiquitous Confusion** (5.12c/d) Right of *Purple Haze*. Awesome. Pockets and extremely thin edges. 5 bolts. FA: Brian Mullin; 9/90.

41. **Purple Haze** (5.11d) Crack on large wall 80' past *The Golden Egg* by aspen grove. Start in crack, and then go right just past the first bolt to the face. 4 bolts. FA: Brian Mullin; 5/90.

42. **Gunk's Pump** (5.11a/b) Left of *Purple Haze*. Climb the crack and pull through a bulge. 4 bolts. FA: Mark Milligan, Bob D'Antonio; 10/90.

43. **Old and Awesome** (5.11d) No topo. 75' north of the *Purple Haze* wall. Crack to high-angled face. 4 bolts. FA: Bob D'Antonio, Mark Milligan; 10/90.

The following climbs are located in a small canyon 450' past the Witch's Eye formation. Go left at the small rock ledge for 200' up a dry creekbed. The routes are on the right. No topos.

44. **Powerfinger** (5.11c) A long, curved fin at the end of the dry streambed. 3 bolts. FA: Brian Mullin; 4/91

45. **A Deal with the Devil** (5.12b) An overhanging wall with bolts just left of *Powerfinger*. 4 bolts. FA: Bob D'Antonio; 5/91.

46. **Hung Low** (5.12b) Find a large dead tree over the creekbed. Hard moves up a steep wall with the crux at the top. 4 bolts. FA: Brian Mullin?; 9/91.

47. **Backward Seven** (5.12b) A fine route 50' past *Hung Low*. 3 bolts and gear. FA: Brian Mullin; 10/91.

48. **Rust Never Sleeps** (5.11c) But does Neil Young? A crack leads to a bulge. Across the creekbed from *Egotonio*. 3 bolts. FA: Brian Mullin; 6/91.

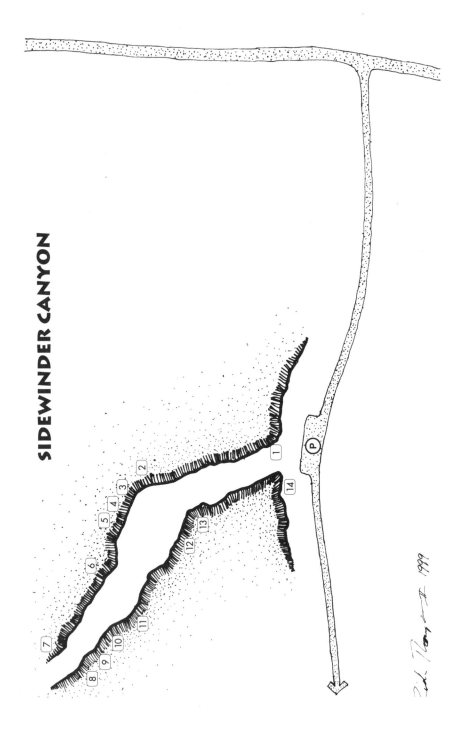

SIDEWINDER CANYON

SIDEWINDER CANYON

If you're looking for some real isolation and cool climbing, Sidewinder Canyon is the place to visit. It is one of the more remote canyons around this part of the San Luis Valley. A short hike up the canyon from the parking area easily accesses most of the routes. Sidewinder is a fairly small canyon with only a few cliffs tall enough for routes. Most of the walls tend to be isolated from each other, but finding the routes is relatively easy. Routes are oriented north and south, so Sidewinder is a great place to beat the summer heat. Some of the best rock in the region is on the Mudhoney Wall.

Finding the canyon: Drive a mile west from the La Garita Cash Store, keeping left at the main junction onto Saguache County 38, to the turnoff for Penitente (marked with a sign). Zero your odometer here and continue south on County 38. Look for the sign marking Sidewinder Canyon on the right side of the road at about 0.7 mile. Turn west on this rough road, veering left at 1.5 miles and going up and over the hill. At about 2.1 miles and the bottom of the hill, take the west road instead of the main southerly road. At 2.8 miles, the small canyon on your right is Sidewinder Canyon. The road continues on for a few hundred feet up the main canyon. The road to Sidewinder is a bit rough, but two-wheel-drive vehicles can make it.

1. **Helen Keller Plaid** (5.11c) Near right side of the road at the start of the canyon. Small angled arête. 3 bolts. FA: Brian Mullin; 7/90.

2. **Pygmy Love Circus** (5.10c) Located 800' up the canyon. First route on north side, right of a large roof. 3 bolts. FA: Brian Mullin, Melanie Tuttle; 6/90.

3. **Snakehead** (5.11c/d) The route starts left of a large roof that looks like a large snake's head, hence the name. 4 bolts. FA: Brian Mullin; 5/90.

4. **Johnny Lead Fingers** (5.11c) Next wall, just left of *Snakehead*. Arête start. 4 bolts. FA: Brian Mullin; 5/90.

5. **Liquid Sky** (5.11c/d) Left of *Lead Fingers* on same wall. Slab leading up to pretty face. 4 bolts. FA: Brian Mullin; 5/90.

6. **Vivian Section** (5.11d) Next wall left of *Liquid Sky*. 3 bolts. FA: Brian Mullin; 5/90.

7. **Auntie Winnie** (5.11c/d) North side of the canyon 600' west of *Snakehead*. 3 bolts. FA: Brian Mullin; 6/90.

8. **Rubber Room** (5.11c) Don't bounce off the wall on this one. Third route right of *Mudhoney*. Follow ramp to start. 3 bolts. FA: Brian Mullin; 4/91.

9. **Spiderbaby** (5.12a/b) The second best route in the canyon. A Valley classic. Second route right of *Mudhoney*. 5 bolts. FA: Brian Mullin; 6/90.

10. **Hallucinations Of Grandeur** (5.12a) Another classic route with excellent rock. First route right of *Mudhoney*. A short, thin crux at the start gives way to two big holds near the top. 5 bolts. FA: Brian Mullin; 5/90.

11. **Mudhoney** (5.13a) A beautiful route with almost perfect rock. 350' west of *Snakehead* on the south side of canyon. Swing up the obvious, overhanging, pocketed face. 5 bolts. FA: Brian Mullin; 5/91.

12. **Trotsky Icepick** (5.11c/d) Right of *Jesus Lizard*. A thin, hard crux leads up to bigger holds and an easy finish. 3 bolts. FA: Brian Mullin, Melanie Tuttle; 6/90.

13. **Jesus Lizard** (5.11b/c) Left-hand route on the south side of canyon, across from *Snakehead*. 4 bolts. FA: Brian Mullin, Melanie Tuttle; 5/90.

14. **Pumped for Allah** (5.12a) Left side at the start of the canyon. A short, strenuous heel hook roof leads to face moves and easier ground. 4 bolts. FA: Brian Mullin; 8/90.

PENIS ROCK

Penis Rock, named for the formation's obvious phallic shape, is an excellent, off-the-beaten-track pinnacle tucked away in a hidden side canyon south of Penitente Canyon. This remote, detached pinnacle is a wonder of random erosion. The views from the summit of the spire east to the Sangre de Cristo Mountains are incredible. There are a few worthwhile routes in the canyon below the rock, but Penis Rock is the must-see and must-climb attraction. Some great bouldering can also be found in the immediate area.

The area around Penis Rock is remote and beautiful. You won't see many people wandering around back there. The area is great for hiking and mountain biking with many old four-wheel-drive roads crisscrossing the rough land. Hikers around Penis Rock often see hawks, coyotes, elk, and deer. So if you are looking for something exciting to do on a rest day, go out and explore the beautiful backcountry around Penis Rock.

Finding the pinnacle: Drive a mile west from the La Garita Cash Store, keeping left at the main junction onto Saguache County 38, to the turnoff for Penitente Canyon (marked with a sign). Zero your odometer here and continue south on County 38. At 0.7 mile, look for the sign for Sidewinder Canyon on your right. Turn right (west) on the dirt road just past the sign. At 1.5 miles, veer left and continue up and over a hill. At about 2.1 miles and the bottom of a hill, take the main road south. Drive up and over another hill to a dry gulch. At about 3.1 miles, keep right and drive until your odometer reads 3.6 miles. Park here and hike due west for 0.5 mile up a hill to the rock. The road is a bit rough, but two-wheel-drive cars can usually make it with care.

1. **Barefoot in the Head** (5.11c) In the canyon where you park (at mile 3.6). This is the first route in the canyon on the east end of cliffs, which face south. Arête to face. 4 bolts. FA: Brian Mullin; 8/90.

2. **Unknown** (5.11/5.12) Quarter-mile west of *Barefoot* on the same cliff band. 4 bolts. FA: Glen Schuler; 90.

3. **Soul Pole** (5.11d) Up the east side of Penis Rock. Laybacks and huecos to multiple slab and face combinations. Incredible position. Awesome view on top. Just do it! 6 bolts. FA: Brian Mullin; 3/90.

4. **Half a Man** (5.11d) On Penis Rock, right of *Soul Pole*. Hard moves with groundfall potential—watch the clips and don't fall. Old loose bolts. 3 bolts. FA: Bob D'Antonio; 3/85.

5. **Happenis** (5.10 R) On Penis Rock. Up a thin crack to a bolt, somewhat runout. 1 bolt. FA: Kevin Lindorff; 84.

6. **Shelf Expression** (5.7) Back side of Penis Rock pinnacle. Rack: Medium gear. FA: Mark Hoffman; 7/85.

LA GARITA CREEK WALL

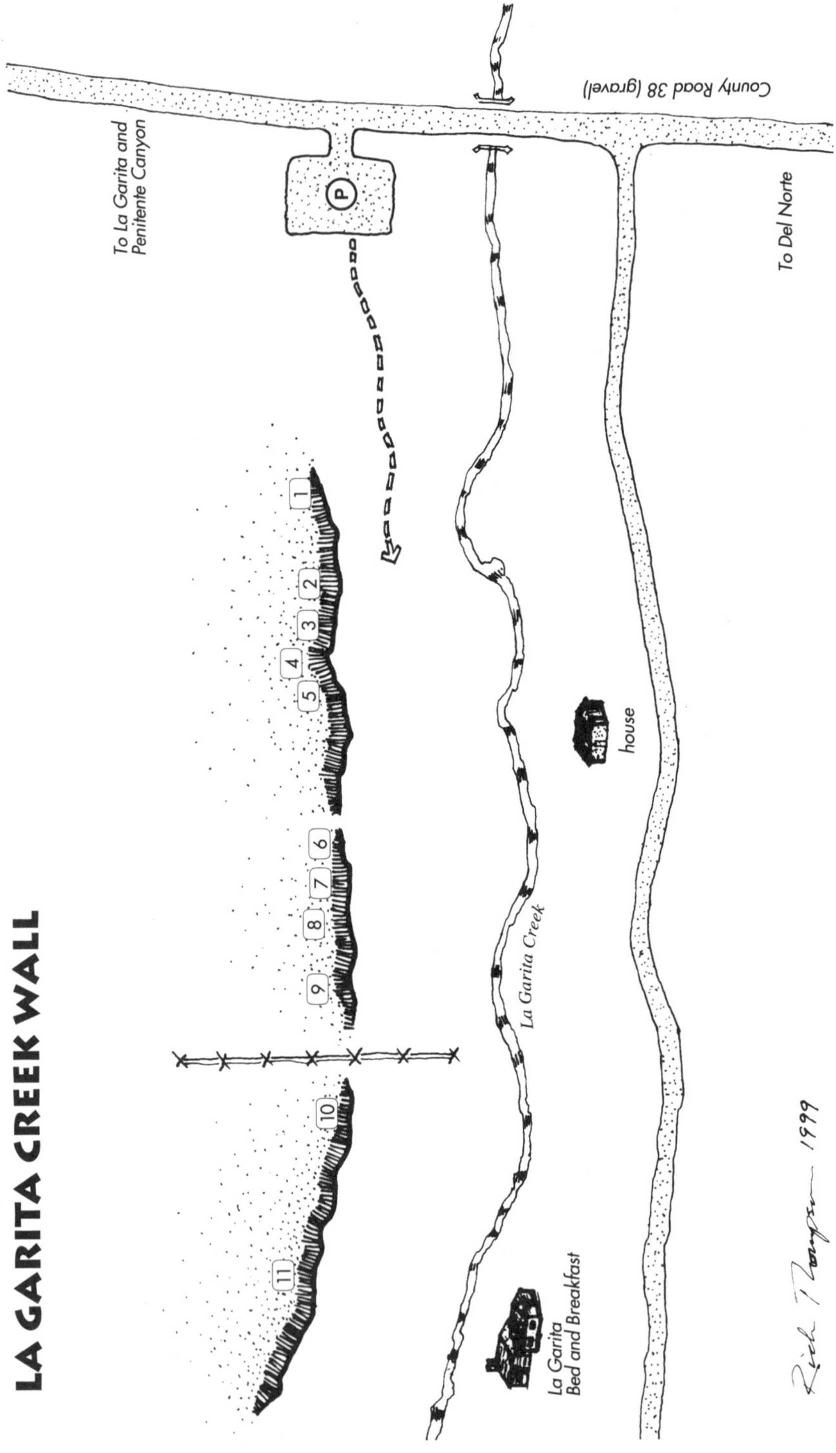

To La Garita and
Penitente Canyon

County Road 38 (gravel)

To Del Norte

P

house

La Garita Creek

La Garita
Bed and Breakfast

1
2
3
4
5
6
7
8
9
10
11

Rick Thompson 1999

LA GARITA CREEK WALL

La Garita Creek Wall is a wonderful place to climb and hang out. The routes offer a mixture of pockets and edges as well as superb crack climbing on quality rhyolite. Be prepared for some vicious stemming routes up excellent corners. Some of the best routes in the San Luis Valley are on this cliff, making it a must stop for visiting climbers. Keep a low profile and take care of the cliff and the surrounding lands. Please respect the wishes of the landowners whose lands surround the cliff—La Garita Bed & Breakfast and the Hick family. The surrounding views of the Sangre de Cristo Mountains and Del Norte Peak are nothing short of spectacular. For those of you who fish, La Garita Creek offers excellent trout fishing just below the cliffs. Owls, hawks, and other birds of prey call the cliff their home. Be respectful to these and all the animals that inhabit this lovely area.

Finding the wall: Drive a mile west from the La Garita Cash Store, keeping left at the main junction onto Saquache County 38, to the turnoff for Penitente Canyon (marked with a sign). Zero your odometer here and continue south on County 38 toward Del Norte. Drive southwest from this fork for 1.5 miles to a BLM horse corral. Park your car here and follow a trail that accesses La Garita Creek and the start of the cliff. The climbs are described right to left (east to west), with Route 1 on the far eastern part of the cliff and Route 11 on the far western part of the cliff.

1. **Life with Mike** (5.11c) Climb an overhanging corner to a big ledge. Follow a thin crack with bad gear to the top and safety—whew! Rack: RPs and camming gear. FA: Bob D'Antonio, Mike Kennedy; 7/86.

2. **I Seen Sex** (5.12a) So what does it look like? Find an overhanging corner with an old fixed piton and a fixed RP. Rack: Wires, TCUs, and cams to #2 Friend. FA: Bob D'Antonio; 7/85.

3. **RFM (Rapid Finger Movement)** (5.12d/5.13a) Excellent! Keep those fingers moving. Follow a line of bolts up a steep white face. 7 bolts. FA: Bob D'Antonio, Tony Herr; 4/91.

The author climbing pockets, *Once upon a Time in the Valley* (5.12a) at La Garita Creek Wall.

4. **Book of Brilliant Things** (5.12b) One of the best-looking corners around these parts! Stem up the gorgeous, near perfect, left-facing dihedral. The crux is near the top. Rack: TCUs and cams to #2 Friend. FA: Bob D'Antonio; 7/85.

5. A **Stem Too Far** (5.12a) Another excellent stemming problem! You should stretch before doing this one. 5 bolts. FA: Bob D'Antonio, Albert Pisaneschi; 9/91.

6. **Coal Crackers from PA** (5.11c) Great stemming up the corner to the right of *Vision Quest*. 4 bolts. FA: Albert Pisaneschi, Bob D'Antonio; 9/91.

7. **Vision Quest** (5.12c) A Valley classic! A short corner leads up to a beautiful face and the crux. Do this route. 6 bolts. FA: Bob D'Antonio, Albert Pisaneschi; 9/91.

8. **Once upon a Time in the Valley** (5.12a) The route follows a line of bolts up a beautiful, pocketed face just left of *Vision Quest*. 7 bolts. FA: Bob D'Antonio; 7/91.

9. **Pocket Plethora** (5.11c) Don't miss this route. It's really one of the best in the Valley. The name says it all. 5 bolts. FA: Bob D'Antonio, Jeff Fasset, and Tom Perkins; 5/92.

10. **Blockhead** (5.9) Hand crack 200' left of *Pocket Plethora*. Rack: Gear to #2.5 Friend. FA: Mark Hoffman, Bob D'Antonio; 7/85.

11. **SST** (5.12b) A superb, thin finger and hand crack located 300' west of *Pocket Plethora* at a fence line. The first 5.12 in the San Luis Valley. Rack: Gear to #2.5 Friend. FA: Bob D'Antonio; 6/84.

SHAW SPRINGS LOCATOR MAP

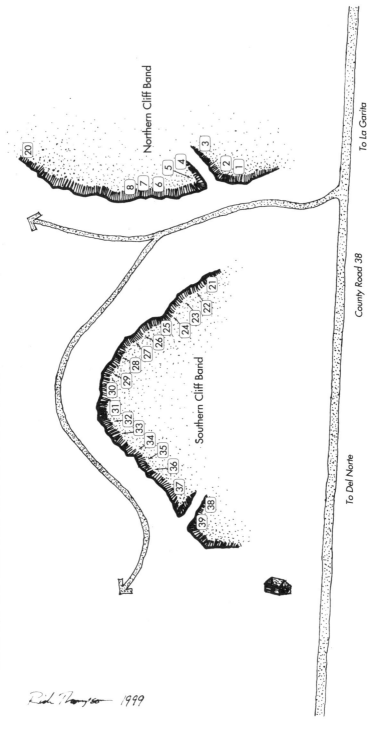

Northern Cliff Band

Southern Cliff Band

To La Garita

County Road 38

To Del Norte

20

8 7 6 5 4 3 2 1

21 22 23 24 25 26 27 28 29 30 31 32 33 34 35 36 37 38 39

Rich Thompson 1999

SHAW SPRINGS

In the late 1800s, Shaw Springs was a hot vacation spot for the rich and famous who came here to relax in the warm water spring. The area is now partially on private land, so please keep a low profile and keep away from the house. Also, please don't add any more routes near the house.

The atmosphere of Shaw Springs is quite different because the cliffs are out in the open rather than tucked into a canyon like other climbing areas on this side of the San Luis Valley. Sometimes it can be windy here, but the cliffs stay in the sun all afternoon, making it a great choice for winter cragging.

There are two main cliff bands, and almost all of the routes face southwest. Shaw Springs has never been as popular with climbers as the other Valley cliffs because the rock tends to be more friable and rotten than that of the other crags. There are some worthwhile routes here, but the majority of lines lack the quality and consistency of the climbing in nearby Penitente Canyon and the Rock Garden.

Bring some gear for climbing at Shaw Springs because there are a number of excellent crack routes that take natural gear. A good selection of camming units and small nuts will suffice on most of the crack routes. If you are looking to do some quality traditional routes, I recommend *The Book*, *In God's Country*, *Hawkeye*, and *Bosch H-Factor*.

Finding the cliffs: Drive a mile west from the La Garita Cash Store on Saguache County 38, keeping left at the main junction, to the turnoff for Penitente Canyon (marked with a sign). Zero your odometer here and continue south on County 38. Access the northern set of cliffs by turning west on the dirt road just before a big pile of dirt and a road reflector at 6.2 miles. Drive in about 0.5 mile. Access the southern set of cliffs (closer to the house) by turning west by the 40 mph speed limit sign (it faces south) at 6.5 miles and driving west until 7.5 miles. Bear left at the T-intersection and drive until 7.7 miles. Bear right onto the road that parallels the cliffs. Park here.

NORTHERN CLIFF BAND

1. **What's a Meat Puppet?** (5.12a/b) A great line. Blank face across the canyon from an openbook crack. 4 bolts. FA: Brian Mullin; 5/89.

2. **Liquid Love** (5.11b) Left of *Meat Puppet*. 2 bolts. FA: Brian Mullin; 8/89.

3. **Varicose Pop Tart** (5.11a) Located 60' left of *Meat Puppet*. Crack to arête. Pretty rock and line. 3 bolts. FA: Brian Mullin; 7/89.

4. **The Book** (5.11c) Obvious openbook on the southeast face of the cliffs. Crack with roof. Rack: Medium to large Friends. FA: Richard Aschert, Ed Pearsall; 5/87.

5. **Throne of Blood** (5.11d) Short route left of openbook crack. Corner to bulge. 3 bolts. FA: Brian Mullin; 11/88.

6. **Bosch H-Factor** (5.12+) Obvious black-streaked wall 250' left of *The Book*. 2 bolts. **Rack:** RPs. FA: Bob D'Antonio, Richard Aschert; 5/87.

7a. **In God's Country** (5.10c) Obvious hand crack out a small roof. Rack: Cams to #2.5 Friend. FA: Ed Pearsall, Bob D'Antonio; 5/87.

7b. **Beaver Cleaver** (5.11b) Lies 75' left of *Bosch H-Factor*. 5 bolts. FA: Brian Mullin; 9/89.

8. **Transparent Radiation** (5.11c) Start 50' right of *Venus*. Face to slab finish. Awesome. 5 bolts. FA Brian Mullin; 9/89.

9. **Venus Groovepusher** (5.12d) Middle of cliffs. White quartz lines the groove. Finger ripper. 6 bolts. FA: Brian Mullin; 11/89.

10. **Lubricating the Species** (5.12a) Begin 100' left of *Venus*. Start on upper loose slab. Pull to arête. 4 bolts. FA: Brian Mullin; 9/89.

11. **Short but Hard** (5.12) Located 175' left of *Venus*. Is this route a joke? 2 bolts. FA: Brian Mullin; 7/89.

12. **Vanilla Chainsaw** (5.11d) Lies 250' left of *Venus*. Overhang to face. 4 bolts. FA: Brian Mullin; 9/89.

13. **Surfing in a Dust Storm** (5.12c/d) Located 200' right of *Zodiac*. Left of obvious butt crack. Overhang to face, horizontal crack. 3 bolts Rack: Large TCUs. FA: Brian Mullin; 3/89.

14. **Surf Combat** (5.11c) Just right of *Zodiac*. Crack in corner to roof. 3 bolts. FA: Brian Mullin; 6/89.

15. **Zodiac Mindwarp** (5.10b) West-facing route just where the cliffs go north. Crack and face. Rack: Medium TCU. 2 bolts. FA: Brian Mullin; 3/89.

16. **Playdoh Meathook** (5.11a) Begin 40' left of *Zodiac* in alcove. Crack/dihedral. 3 bolts. FA: Brian Mullin; 8/89.

17. **Ripping Tendons** (5.12c) Left of *Playdoh Meathook*. Strenuous face climbing. The name says it all. 4 bolts. FA: Brian Mullin, Charles Walters; 6/89.

18. **Lithium Christmas** (5.12a) Left of *Ripping Tendons*. Sidepull finish. 3 bolts. FA: Brian Mullin; 8/89.

19. **Asphalt Metal Locusts** (5.12a/b) Left of *Lithium*. Edges to bulge to slab. 4 bolts. FA: Brian Mullin; 9/89.

20. **Brain Drops** (5.11d) Start 150' left of *Asphalt*. Corner to arête with face. 4 bolts. FA: Brian Mullin; 10/89.

SOUTHERN CLIFF BAND

21. **Hot Pink** (5.9) First route at the north end of the cliffs. Face and crack. 3 bolts. FA: Charles Walters, Brian Mullin; 89.

22. **Misguided Angel** (5.11d) Right of *Hot Pink*. Hard boulder start. 4 bolts. FA: Brian Mullin; 9/89.

23. **Experience the Pain** (5.12c) Located 100' right of *Angel*. Extremely hard face. A tendon and skin ripper route—be prepared for pain and suffering. 6 bolts. FA: Brian Mullin; 4/89.

24. **Speed Demon** (5.11d) 30 feet right of *Experience the Pain*. 4 bolts. FA: Brian Mullin; 1/89.

25. **Eternal Thirst** (5.11c/d) Right of *Speed Demon*. Balance/thin start. 4 bolts. FA: Brian Mullin; 10/89.

26. **The Fire Inside** (5.11a) Lies 100 feet right of *Eternal Thirst*. Fine route. 4 bolts. FA: Jack Hunt, Norm Slade; 11/91.

27. **One-Eyed Hose Monster** (5.12a/b) Start 175' right of *Eternal Thirst* by some small trees. Excellent long pitch. Thin bulge start to thinner face and a great juggy finish. 7 bolts. FA: Brian Mullin; 11/89.

28. **Sonic Reducer** (5.11c/d) 80 feet right of *One-Eyed*. Neat trough line, but a bit flaky. 4 bolts. FA: Brian Mullin; 8/89.

29. **Take Off Your Skin** (5.12b) Right of *Sonic Reducer*. Multiple bulges. Strenuous and long. 7 bolts. FA: Brian Mullin; 7/89.

30. **Hawkeye** (5.11a/b) Left of *Swallow*. Great stemming crack. Rack: Small to medium TCUs. FA: Bob D'Antonio, Ed Pearsall; 5/87.

31. **Swallow My Pride** (5.12c) Lies 30' left of *Prairie*. Crack to face to a hard bulge. Run-out finish. 4 bolts. FA: Brian Mullin; 10/89.

32. **Prairie School Freakout** (5.11c) Obvious red and brown, hueco/dish wall with X-shaped crack system. 3 bolts. FA: Brian Mullin; 11/88.

33. **Insatiable Desires** (5.11d) Right of *Prairie*. Hard arête start to face. 5 bolts. FA: Brian Mullin; 10/89.

34. **Rearranging the Atmosphere** (5.12b) Second route right of *Prairie*. Cold shuts. 5 bolts. FA: Brian Mullin; 7/89

35. **Mr. Zig Zag Man** (5.11d) Obvious Z-crack near the house end of cliffs. Dihedral and face. 5 bolts. Rack: TCUs. FA: Brian Mullin, Charles Walters; 11/88.

36. **Controlled Bleeding** (5.11d) Begin 40' right of *Mr. Zig Zag Man*. Great reachy edges. 6 bolts. FA: Brian Mullin; 11/89.

37. **High Plains Drifter** (5.11c/d) Just before main cliffs turn north by house. Boulder start. 5 bolts. FA: Brian Mullin; 10/89.

38. **Lexicon Devil** (5.10a) Across from *Muffin*. Crack to ledge. 1 bolt. Rack: Small to medium TCUs. FA: Brian Mullin; 7/89.

39. **Electric Love Muffin** (5.11d) Southwest-facing wall inside the canyon and facing the house. 4 bolts. FA: Brian Mullin; 5/89.

Bouldering in the San Luis Valley

Bouldering lies at the very heart and soul of climbing. It's just the climber and the rock. Standards achieved on today's hardest roped routes were reached years before on the boulders. The San Luis Valley is no exception. The Valley offers many magical and mostly isolated locales for bouldering away an afternoon. Out here, climbers can discover the joys of bouldering by roaming through canyons and over ridges in search of stellar boulder problems that may or may not have been climbed before—adventure bouldering at its finest. The following is only a small sampling of the bouldering potential that exists in the Valley. Come and climb, and I hope you enjoy these boulders as much as I have.

This short chapter gives directions to some of the best San Luis Valley bouldering areas. But first, a short history. Lew Hoffman provided the following introduction:

> After learning the ropes at the Tetons' Exum school in 1977, I stumbled onto bouldering by practicing on the excellent granite outcrops near Ortonville, Minnesota. A few visits to the Black Hills, featuring tours of John Gill problems by locals Kevin Bein and his wife Barbara Devine, hooked me on bouldering as an end in its own right.
>
> After moving to the Valley in August 1979, I met and bouldered often with John Gill, and with the benefit of his example sought to transfer some of his approach to my own efforts on the limitless Valley rhyolite.
>
> I first met Bob D'Antonio at the Garden of the Gods on New Years Day, 1984. His on-sight abilities on his first Valley visit set the stage for future sport climbing developments—which I call "linked-lead bouldering." D'Antonio and his friend Bob Murray visited throughout the mid-1980s. Murray's studied, athletic prowess bagged many undone plums. This area is far from being bouldered out. There are many areas whose potential has been barely tapped. For the boulderer who is looking for real solitude, the San Luis Valley just might be the place to be.

CROCODILE ROCK

This boulder is in The Rock Garden. Find this fine piece of rhyolite 200' up the hill (east) from *You're Busted*. Watch out, it does bite.

BALLOON RANCH BOULDERS

Dozens of world-class boulders, with mostly kind landings, await the infrequent visitor. On the most outrageous dynamic problems, you may find a speck of chalk left by Bob Murray a decade ago.

Finding the boulders: Follow directions to Penis Rock. Cross a dry gulch at 3.9 miles from the main road. Instead of going right to Penis Rock, go uphill for 0.6 mile to the boulders on the right. This area is extensive. The views east across the San Luis Valley to the Sangre de Cristo Range are amazing!

EAGLE ROCK

Numerous free-standing boulders composed of breccia scatter across slopes below the south face of Eagle Rock. Bob Murray found these rocks well suited to his talents.

Finding the boulders: Drive 2.5 miles south on Saguache County 38 from the turnoff to Penitente. Take a right (west) on Forest Service Road 660 and drive 3.5 miles, until you're directly south of Eagle Rock, a massive south-facing buttress. Hike cross-country for 10 minutes to the obvious boulders on the slopes below the cliff.

ELEPHANT ROCKS

This extensive area of boulders and small faces eroding out of a ridge offers days of exploration for the hardcore boulderer in search of new, off-the-beaten-track problems. The best boulders found so far are the Shaw Springs Boulders and the far southern end of the Elephant Rocks.

Finding the boulders: Drive 6.3 miles south from the turnoff to Penitente on Saguache County 38 toward Del Norte. Turn right (west) and drive 0.5 mile to the boulders.

COURTHOUSE BOULDERS

Urban bouldering in the town of Del Norte. A few excellent dynamic problems. Worth a visit if you are in the area.

Finding the bouldering: From the only traffic light in town, head two blocks south and half a block east to the county courthouse.

HIDDEN GULCH

Great bouldering in a remote setting. Go with another person—this not the place to be by yourself if you happen to get hurt.

Finding the boulders: From the stoplight in Del Norte, drive east on U.S. Highway 160 for 4.2 miles. Turn south (right) on a road onto BLM land and wind southwest along the dirt road for a few miles to a fence line. Drive a few hundred yards farther and park in the sandy outlet of Hidden Gulch. Walk up the dry streambed to the boulders.

BREAKFAST BOULDERS

This is my favorite bouldering spot in the San Luis Valley. Bring a few beers and enjoy a mellow afternoon bouldering on the Split Egg and the Yolk in a beautiful meadow surrounded by aspens. This place is well worth the drive. Also, there is roped climbing located at Big Meadows just before the start of Wolf Creek Pass on US Highway 160.

Finding the boulders: This area is west of the San Luis Valley itself. Drive west from Del Norte on US Highway 160 to the town of South Fork. At the Y-junction in South Fork, keep left (west) on US 160. At 1.4 miles from the fork, turn left on Forest Service Road 360 (access to Beaver Creek) and drive 1.4 miles to Million Reservoir. Turn left here, drive to the top of a hill, and park at the barbed wire road closure. The Breakfast Boulders are 100 yards southwest in an aspen grove.

RATED ROUTE INDEX

ROUTE NAME INDEX

ACCESS: It's every climber's concern

The Access Fund, a national, non-profit climbers' organization, works to keep climbing areas open and to conserve the climbing environment. Need help with closures? land acquisition? legal or land management issues? funding for trails and other projects? starting a local climbers' group? CALL US!

Climbers can help preserve access by being committed to leaving the environment in its natural state. Here are some simple guidelines:

• **STRIVE FOR ZERO IMPACT** especially in environmentally sensitive areas like caves. Chalk can be a significant impact on dark and porous rock—don't use it around historic rock art. Pick up litter, and leave trees and plants intact.

• **DISPOSE OF HUMAN WASTE PROPERLY** Use toilets whenever possible. If toilets are not available, dig a "cat hole" at least six inches deep and 200 feet from any water, trails, campsites, or the base of climbs. *Always pack out toilet paper.* On big wall routes, use a "poop tube" and carry waste up and off with you (the old "bag toss" is now illegal in many areas).

• **USE EXISTING TRAILS** Cutting switchbacks causes erosion. When walking off-trail, tread lightly, especially in the desert where cryptogamic soils (usually a dark crust) take thousands of years to form and are easily damaged. Be aware that "rim ecologies" (the clifftop) are often highly sensitive to disturbance.

• **BE DISCREET WITH FIXED ANCHORS** *Bolts are controversial and are not a convenience*—don't place 'em unless they are *really* necessary. Camouflage all anchors. Remove unsightly slings from rappel stations (better to use steel chain or welded cold shuts). Bolts sometimes can be used pro-actively to protect fragile resources—consult with your local land manager.

• **RESPECT THE RULES** and speak up when other climbers don't. Expect restrictions in designated wilderness areas, rock art sites, caves, and to protect wildlife, especially nesting birds of prey. *Power drills are illegal in wilderness and all national parks.*

• **PARK AND CAMP IN DESIGNATED AREAS** Some climbing areas require a permit for overnight camping.

• **MAINTAIN A LOW PROFILE** Leave the boom box and day-glo clothing at home—the less climbers are heard and seen, the better.

• **RESPECT PRIVATE PROPERTY** Be courteous to land owners. Don't climb where you're not wanted.

• **JOIN THE ACCESS FUND!** To become a member, make a tax-deductible donation of $25 or more.

The Access Fund

Preserving America's Diverse Climbing Resources
PO Box 17010 Boulder, CO 80308
303.545.6772 • www.accessfund.org